It is Finished

By Peter-John Courson

Dedicated to my wife, Amanda. We both know why.

Preface for the Book

When I was twenty years old I lost my life. The malaria I contracted while living in Vanuatu did not kill me, but there have been days since that I thought it would. And in some ways, even wished it had. My life I had known before I became sick was over. For some unknown reason, the fever brought on by the malaria virus created a domino effect. My immune system, the very thing that was supposed to save me, actually became my enemy as it turned against me and started attacking my digestive system. This was officially diagnosed as Crohn's Disease, but I prefer call it my "thorn in the flesh."

Since returning back from the South Pacific, I have been forty pounds underweight and then forty pounds overweight within a matter of months. I spent afternoons sitting in my car with the heat blasted to the maximum… in August. I took little anti-inflammatories known as "The Devil's Tic Tacs." And I had surgery that left me semi-conscious during the removal of part of my small intestine. That was the first year of having Crohn's. Twenty years later, things have not improved all that much as far as my health is concerned. I am worn out of diets, research, studies, cleanses, and colonoscopies. I have been both the one who prays and has been prayed for far beyond count. I no longer use the restroom like you probably do and lost my job because of a lack of performance. In recent years, there have been seasons where my kids had a dad who was in bed and my wife had to learn to do things like install a sink or pay the bills by herself. I am forty years old and extremely tired. I am learning to rest.

I was made to embark on a journey that I would never have likely volunteered for. It has been the genuine test, one that goes to the very core of who I am. As such, I have come to find a genuine rest. I searched for a rest that was more than physical because I recognized the physical symptoms were a part of a deeper issue. My immune system would not shut down because I felt as though my inner being was not at rest. I knew I needed to find rest from doubt and rest from shame. I needed to find peace away from anger and worry. Most of all, I needed to cease from striving in self-justification.

The harder I have tried to justify myself, the more I have been set back. The less I have tried to justify myself, the more progress I have been able to make. The great paradox of life that I am beginning to discover is that when it comes to justification through self effort; less is more. I can see the truth in Jesus' statement, teaching us that when we lose our true selves in Him that is when we find our true selves through Him. To lose oneself in Christ is by completely placing one's justification in the Finished work of the Cross. The more one embraces the Finished work of the Cross, the less one tries to be. And the more one is just able to be, the more one becomes.

"It is Finished" is the Magnum Opus of the Gospel. It is the Declaration of Independence away from the slavery of self-righteousness. That truth is able to grant the rest found beneath every other rest. There is no location to travel to that will give the soul the rest that the Finished work of the Cross is able to give. You cannot find a friend or lover with the capacity to give your heart the satisfaction that the perfect love of Christ is able to offer. The Finished work of the Cross is so total in its accomplishment, that to add anything to it will only take away from your experience of it. It is the virtuoso work which gives rest to the weary. For I have been able to (begin to) learn that the true secret of life is to not strive in order to become; becoming flows from the freedom of just being. Instead of trying to be something more, the real progress takes place when you are able to just be. That is a freedom afforded nowhere but the Finished work of the Cross. It is not based on our accomplishment, as though we merit the right to just be. It is just the opposite. The very reason we can just be is because of nothing we have accomplished on our own. We find rest in the work of Another.

The more you understand just how "finished" the Finished work of the Cross is, you will be amazed at how much more you are able to do. When you rest in what it means to trust in Christ and just be, you will see new horizons in what you are becoming.

Tetelestai

"It is Finished". The word that the Gospel of John employs in the Greek language is *tetelestai*. It was Jesus' final word before He bowed His head and committed His Spirit into the Father's hands. *Tetelestai* was an economic term at the time of the First Century. It was a word used by Roman officials during tax collection and was stamped on tax receipts to indicate that the debt had been paid in full. It was also a word that was probably used in other occurrences of life in the Roman Empire. *Tetelestai* may have been spoken by an artist upon completing a painting or a project. It may have been a judicial term used to pronounce a prison term had been served. It has been suggested that it may have been the cry of a general upon victory over an enemy on the battlefield. In any case, the term was one that definitively declared something significant had been accomplished. The fact that it was a verb that was cried in the present perfect tense reveals that it was something He meant to be understood as finished once and for all.

In the waning moments of His life, as strength was ebbing from His body, it is very probable that Jesus didn't use His final breath to shout out a statement such as "It is Finished" in a secondary language. His primary, native tongue was not Greek but Aramaic. Therefore, I believe that Jesus made that final cry in the Aramaic language. The Aramaic equivalent to the Greek word *tetelestai* was the word *kalah*. They are essentially the same in their definition and yet there is a nuanced difference in their meaning. While the word *tetelestai* seems to pertain more to an economic term, *kalah* had more religious, ceremonial overtones to it. According to the Mishnah, *kalah* was shouted by the High Priest on the Passover Eve. To the High Priest, the word *kalah* meant that all was complete. For leading up to the moment he made that declaration, tens of thousands of sheep and livestock would be sacrificed on the altars of the Temple in Jerusalem in the week leading up to the Passover. There were so many sheep sacrificed in that particular week that Josephus, a historian from the First Century, writes that the Kidron Brook, the stream running just outside the city gates, would turn crimson due to the flow of blood streaming from the Temple Mount. Therefore, so great was the sense of completion, at the three o'clock hour, which would mark the time of the evening sacrifice, the High Priest would cry *kalah* or "It is Complete." The Gospel account tells us that it was at that very hour in the afternoon that Jesus shouted, "It is Finished." I believe that the *kalah* of the High Priest coincided with that shouted by Jesus. Separated by only a few hundred feet, the High Priest at the top of the Temple Mount and Jesus hanging on the Cross at its base, both simultaneously declared, "It is Finished!"

Whether Jesus shouted "It is Finished" in Greek or Aramaic, John chose the Greek term, *tetelestai,* to chronicle what was spoken that day from the Cross. *Tetelestai* is a word that speaks into our lives in a way that is just as relevant today as when Jesus spoke it. At the root of the word is *telos*, which means the completion of something in its intended purpose. Another way to say it would be that it means something has fulfilled its potential and continues on in that fulfilled potentiality. Greek philosophy devoted much of its energy and attention to the consideration of *telos*. Even to this day, we have an entire branch of philosophy dedicated to the study of *telos*, which would be Teleology. The whole concept revolves around what the purpose of something is.

Each of us are looking for our own "Tetelestai". By that I mean, we are wanting to know that our meaning and purpose is something we are either endeavoring in or something we have already accomplished. Each of us desires to know that "It is Finished" when it comes to who we are and what we are supposed to do. The problem lies in that we do not know exactly what that might mean and even if we did, we don't know how to achieve it. That is what the message of the Finished work of the Cross, declared in the Gospel, is able to give to us. It gives a righteousness that is apart from anything we do and anything we are in ourselves. "Righteousness" is not a word that is limited to doctrine and theology and confined to seminaries and pulpits. Righteousness is something that pertains to the deepest desire of every human being. And that is the desire to know that one is alright. To put in another way, knowing one has an "alright-ness" to them. It is the perpetual satisfaction of the soul that comes from addressing the gnawing sense within that we need to be right. The "tetelestai" of each person is the assurance that one is doing and being what they are supposed to be doing and being. But for "alright-ness" to occur, the problem is that one must be "all right". Without perfection, no matter how many right things one does, it will not be enough to convince the subconscious that one is alright. Therefore, there is a need for an "alright-ness" that is attained apart from what a person does.

In order to sense a righteousness, we naturally endeavor to accomplish it through our actions and behavior. It is what Martin Luther referred to as the "default mode of the human heart." That is, to spend our lives seeking to make our case and justify the space we occupy on this Earth. This mission to justify ourselves through what we do and who we are will inevitably become a matter of comparison and, thus, a universal beauty pageant of sorts. For the only way to demonstrate that one is alright is by being more alright than another. I might not be alright compared to this person, but I sure am compared to that one. CS Lewis pointed out that pride is never in just having something. If it were, there would be nothing to be proud of. What precipitates pride is having more of something than another person has. And that is why the pursuit to prove one is righteous is always accompanies by pride. One cannot aspire to self-righteousness and escape the worst sin of all, which is pride.

What constitutes righteousness will vary from one person to another. Most often, it is culture that will define what makes us alright. For some, the culture places a premium on outward appearance. For others, it may be family or career. It is often religion and morality. The list goes on and on. No matter what it may be, anything that one looks to in order to make that their case and justify their existence is their righteousness. And whatever it takes to accomplish this is their salvation. Which makes anyone endeavoring to achieve their righteousness nothing less than their own savior.

The human dilemma in all of this is there is no arbiter outside of ourselves to say that "it is finished." When and where might one find a final judgment that will say "It is enough", "You are successful"? We try to convince ourselves that we have the authority to declare that to ourselves, yet deep down we know that we are only fooling ourselves. One cannot pronounce one's own self to be righteous and not be delusional. The human conundrum of knowing one needs to be all right yet having no way to getting authentic verification of that is why the tune "I can't get no satisfaction" is a familiar one to us all.

This brings us to the "Good" in the "Good News" of the Gospel. For it declares that there is an "alright-ness" that is rooted in an "All Right-ness." For righteousness is now possible and it comes from what we do or do not do. Further, it is a righteousness that is affirmed outside of ourselves. This righteousness is something that is given to us by God and not something we merit through our own accomplishment. Not only does this level the playing field for all of humanity but it completely takes out the human factor when it comes to the solving of the dilemma for salvation.

The righteousness that is now revealed apart from the works of human effort is based on the accomplishment of Jesus Christ through the Finished work of the Cross. It is righteousness not achieved by us but counted to us. The reason it is counted to us is because it was through the obedience of Jesus and His perfection in doing so that affords us this righteousness. Because Jesus did not sin, He was qualified not only to die for our sins because He would but also because He could. He did not die for His own sin as the rest of us will do. Through the fact that He never sinned, He was able to justify us in taking on our sin in His death on the Cross. The Finished work of the Cross means that Jesus was counted a sinner even though He had never sinned so that we might be counted righteous apart from anything we have done. Righteousness means more than mere exoneration from guilt. It means one has merited the right for blessing and to receive favor. Jesus received what I should have received so that now I receive what Jesus deserves to receive.

Jesus' righteousness is complete and not subject to be altered in any way. Therefore, because it is counted to me, neither can my righteousness be altered nor affected. Nothing we do or do not do can make us any more or less righteous than the righteousness that is counted to us through faith in the Finished work of the Cross. It is Jesus that both attains and maintains the righteousness of those who place their faith in the Finished work of the Cross. From the moment of first belief and going all the way through eternity, when it comes to making my case, I am completely off the hook. The reason is that Jesus hung on that Tree and cried out, once and for all, that I am alright. More than that, I am All Right.

There is a rest that comes from the Finished work of Cross subsequent to knowing that one is righteous. It is the rest for the soul, which the Bible calls "shalom". The invitation of salvation is found in these words of Jesus, "Come to me all who are weary and heavy burdened and I will give you rest for your soul. My yoke is easy and my burden is light." This rest is all encompassing for the invitation extends from the body to the innermost being. It is also known as a "Sabbath" in the Bible. It speaks of a rest that is more than a mere day out of the week, but condition of the soul that finds its rest in having the security of no longer striving for righteousness. Jesus' invitation gives permission to rest from trying to be and allows one the freedom just to be.

No one will give you the freedom to just be like Jesus will. The world we live in will demand you justify yourself and make your case to why you should be accepted as you. Jesus Himself was tempted to make His own case when the Devil tempted Him in the desert to turn stones into bread. Not long after that demand by the Devil, Jesus would later create bread supernaturally. However, He did this not to demonstrate Who He was or make a case for Himself, but to meet the needs of thousands of hungry people that were following Him in Galilee. When it came to creating bread in order to prove Himself as the

Son of God, like Satan was demanding, Jesus' response to that demand was to do nothing at all. He was so secure in His righteousness as the Beloved, that he refused every hoop the Devil placed before Him to jump through. Three years later, while hanging on the Cross, the same demand that He demonstrate that He was the Son of God was hurled His way by those mocking Him. As He did with the Devil, so He did with them, which was nothing. He allowed God to justify Him when God raised Him from the dead three days later.

Throughout the course of any given day, The Finished work of the Cross will allow you to rest whenever the Devil, the world, or even our inner-self demand that you do something in order to prove yourself. The Gospel preaches that there is nothing left for you to prove! The sign that Jesus gave for validation of both His and, as a result, ours, was His rising from the dead. The sign of your righteousness being fully secure has nothing to do with what you have accomplished. Jesus literally met every demand that any and all righteousness requires so that the only demand you are under is one that you unnecessarily place upon yourself. The best thing to do in order to prove you are righteous is to do nothing at all, save placing your entire trust in the Finished work of the Cross. We rest in His work.

We will end up doing more when we know that we need do nothing at all. I call this the "reverse psychology of grace." When Peter was focused on Jesus' feet and not his own, Peter lost all inhibition that stems from self-consciousness and followed Jesus out onto the water. When His focus was singularly on what Jesus was doing, Peter was able to do the same. It was only after Peter diverted his attention off of Jesus' walk and was conscious of his own that Peter's own walk suffered and he sank. When Jesus walked on the water, He was foreshadowing an even greater miracle that was to come, the hour He would trample upon death. Jesus' walk was so complete, that though He was plunged into the depths of death, He stepped upon that which all others had been swallowed up in. Through plunging into death and then rising above it, Jesus overcame death. In this accomplishment, He beckons us to do the same. We called by Jesus to step out of the safety of our own self-righteous endeavors and keep our focus on Him. Whether we transcend the sea of our surroundings or sink into it, we will not drown. This is because our righteousness is not secure in our walk but in His. The irony of Peter's walking on the water was that He walked like Jesus walked when he wasn't trying to.

By focusing on the Finished work of the Cross, we become more like Jesus by surprise. It is holiness by accident, in a certain sense. It is definitely a grace that works. The key to the Christian life, one that steps out and moves ahead is not in trying to be a Christian in realizing that one already is.

The Gospel Road

Johnny Cash rightly called it "The Gospel Road". It is the journey of Scripture that leads to the Finished work of the Cross and one that is step by step walked alongside of Jesus. The Gospel Road begins in the Garden of Eden. From there, the road winds its way through Calvary, ultimately ending in the Garden of Eden once again.

Another name for "The Gospel Road" might be "The Road to Emmaus". That was the road Jesus took with two of His disciples after He had risen from the dead. It was a journey of seven miles, heading out of Jerusalem. The two had not recognized it was Jesus Who had joined them on their walk. He asked why they were so obviously perplexed and they basically asked him if He had been under a rock. Which of course, He had, and therefore, took the entire seven miles to explain to them why the Messiah would have to die and rise from the dead. He used the entire Torah to make His case, showing them from beginning to end, who the Bible found the meaning to Its message in the Resurrection of the Christ.

After they were seated and eating, the disciples finally recognized just Who was explaining the Scriptures to them. Just as soon as they realized it was Jesus Who was with them, He was gone from their presence. They said to each other, "No wonder our hearts burned inside as He taught us from the Scriptures." Now that is a Bible Study I simply must have the Podcast for! Notice, they understood the message and the One Whom the message centered around once they were seated and breaking bread at the table. Like those two travelers, we find that as we look to the Finished work of the Cross to be the central theme of all the Bible, we will be seated and rested within our souls, even as our spirits burn with us.

The reading and studying of the Bible is an Emmaus Road experience. It leads us to the place of rest. The entire narrative of the Bible is a quest for rest. Scripture is not an eclectic, discombobulated accumulation of writings. Rather, it is a single storyline and when you know what that storyline is, you are able to become a great expositor in any passage of the Bible. The storyline is how God brings all of humanity back, full circle, from Eden to Eden and rest to rest. It finds its apex when Jesus turned to the thief on the Cross and summed up the entire storyline by saying, "Today you will be with me in Paradise." Truly Paradise is the place of reading the Bible and realizing how complete and total the Finished work of the Cross really is.

The "It" within "It is Finished" is the point of the whole narrative of Scripture. "It" is where all of history and humanity are headed. Rest and righteousness are where the journey on the Gospel Road will ultimately will bring us to. I have marked seven places in the Bible that stand out to me along the way. I call them "rest stops" because in the journey of Scripture, each poignantly illustrates the Finished work of the Cross. Further, each gives us practical insight to how the Finished work of the Cross is able to impact and bless areas of our everyday lives. They deal with spiritual growth, family, career, economics, and emotional centeredness. These "rest stops" are written in no particular order but I trust that you will find further application and even think about what other places in the Bible are "Rest Stops."

I call these seven places, "Rest Stops", because the Sabbath is all about rest. As we shall see in our journey, the Sabbath is more than a day of rest; it is also a way of life. This Sabbath rest for the soul is portrayed in several different ways, depending on the "Rest Stop." It is a collage of pictures such as a king's throne, a fish cooked over coals, a giant, flowing zoo, and a garden. It all pertains to the Day that Jesus completed the work of the Cross and gave us rest by rising on Sunday.

Sometimes when I try to run a sermon point by my kids, basically using them as a test audience, lately the common response has been, "Save it for Sunday, Dad." So, true to nature and following their instruction, I used that very phrase as a Sunday morning message. Jesus' resurrection effectively changed the Sabbath day from Saturday to Sunday for those billions of people around the world. The invitation that Jesus gives to us, a rest for the soul, shows us that God took the entire storyline of the Bible and did exactly what my kids said should be done. He saved it for Sunday.

Rest Stop 1: The Table of the Lord

The Table of the Lord is a meal that is prepared and available through the Finished work of the Cross. Throughout the Bible we see the invitation to come and eat. Wisdom set out her meal in the book of Proverbs. David set a place at his table for the crippled son of his friend. It was at a prepared meal that Esther saved her people from Haman. And Psalm 23 tells us that our Shepherd has "prepared a table for me in the midst of my enemies." The Table is a place to come and find rest. The rest for the soul that is available at Communion, as we eat the bread and drink from the cup, comes from a quiet conscience.

The Finished work of the Cross is able to quiet one's conscience. Ever since Adam and Eve had their eyes opened at the Tree of the Knowledge of Good and Evil, the innermost being of every person generally has awareness that we are neither what we once were, nor should be. It is our conscience that reminds us of this. The deepest part of us needs something to speak into our conscience that we are innocent. Such innocence would be a return to the Garden of Eden, a state of being apart from one's eyes opened and focused on one's self. It is through the Finished work of the Cross, what the Bible refers to as a "perfect conscience" is given. This is because something is finally able to tell the conscience that sin has been forgiven and the debt has been paid. The Cross is able to declare to the conscience, "It is Finished!"

The Holy of Holies was the quietest part of the Temple. The Outer Court of the Temple was one that was bustling with activity everyday. With various parts of it sectioned off for women and Gentiles, crowds of people from all over the world would make their way into the Outer Court to offer sacrifices, make prayers, and listen to various teachings. Inside the

Temple, behind the doors, was the Holy Place. It had considerably less daily activity and yet everyday the priests would make their way into the Holy Place for the ministerial duties there. The lighting of the candle, the setting out of the bread, and the igniting of incense would all be done by the priests in the Holy Place. It was behind the massive veil at the end of the Holy Place where no activity took place at all. There was no human presence in the Holy of Holies, the area of the Temple that was behind the veil. The Ark of the Covenant was located in the Holy of Holies with the Presence of God resting above it. So while the Outer Court was very busy and the Holy Place had activity, all was quiet in the Holy of Holies. The one exception would be on the Day of Atonement. That was the Day heading into the New Year that was dedicated to the forgiveness of the nation's sins. On that Day, the High Priest would take the blood from the altar in the Outer Court and bring it behind the veil into the Holy of Holies. Once there, he would sprinkle the blood on the Mercy Seat, the lid of the Ark of the Covenant, in an act of covering on behalf of the entire Nation of Israel. Once he emerged from that act and stood before the people again, it would become one of the most celebratory moments in all of the yearly Feasts of Israel. The people would have assurance going into the New Year that their sin had been covered and forgiven. This would grant them expectation for blessing and prosperity in the year to come. They were so thrilled to see the High Priest on that Day, the Mishna states that the priest could not tarry too long in the Holy of Holies lest the people grow concerned that he had not survived his encounter with God's presence. They needed to be assured their sins were forgiven and his very presence out of the Holy of Holies was what gave them just that. The Finished work of the Cross proved effective when our High Priest, Jesus

Christ, reemerged from the grave, having gone into Heaven and presented His blood to the justice of God. Once and for all, the declaration has been made that there is nothing more for us to do in order to gain righteousness. A perfect conscience is one that finds its rest in that declaration. And as with the Temple, we may be engaged in all kinds of activity outwardly, but inwardly we have a rest that comes from a conscience that has been quieted by the Blood.

The Bible does not say to "let your conscience be your guide." That is advice given to us by a singing grasshopper wearing a top hat. If you were to follow that advice, you may very well end up in a mental institution. What the Bible does teach is that while your conscience may be a good helper it is a harsh master. Whenever negative connotations are associated with the conscience in the Bible, when such phrases as "seared, defiled, sinful, evil" are used, it has always pertains to self effort and striving to appease the conscience apart from the Finished work of the Cross. The only way one might have a "perfect" conscience is through the sprinkling of the Blood upon it, according to the Book of Hebrews. Any other conscience is a "sinful" conscience and results in "dead works". The reason is that when one engages in works in order to appease their conscience, those very works are then tainted and are not pure in motivation. They are a result of compensating for sin or failure and are thus self serving at their foundation. They become nothing more that a mission of self righteousness, for they do not proceed from a pure conscience.

What the Bible refers to as a "pure" conscience, one that has zero ulterior motives or hidden agendas, can only stem from a "perfect" conscience. It is in resting in the Finished work of the Cross that the conscience finally finds its perfection and becomes still. Without a quiet conscience we act out in all kinds of restless ways. The works of the flesh, as described in Galatians 5, are essentially what we would call neurotic behavior in today's vernacular. All kinds of ugly behavior is described in that text, in contrast with the beauty of the Fruit of the Spirit, found in the same text. The reason the works of the flesh, with all of its arrogant and obnoxious results, are manifest apart from the Fruit of the Spirit is because they are symptomatic of a restless or "evil" conscience. When one is at war with their own conscience, one is at war with one's self. Being in an internal civil war will only sabotage relationships and skew patterns of behavior.

The Blood of Jesus is able to speak peace in the Holy of Holies within you and I and declare a cease-fire with your conscience. Under the Old Covenant, the blood of lambs and goats would temporarily speak to the conscience of the sinner that they were forgiven. But that state of innocence only lasted until the next sin. Now, having a sacrifice made once-and-for-all means we have a perpetual rest within. Our sins that were committed, are being committed, and will be committed have all been atoned for. When it comes to sin, it is a huge undertaking to quiet the conscience. How does one genuinely know when they are sinning or not sinning? Jesus took the Law of Moses to its natural conclusion, when He stated the real issue with the Law is that it is a matter of the heart and not mere outward behavior. Your sin is more than just your behavior, that is, your external actions. It is also the foundations, the soil, and all the components that go on underneath said actions. So does one really know all their sins, all the time? Take motives for example. How does one know if the motive is even slightly tainted with self-centeredness or not? How does one truly know if their thought has missed the mark? In other words, can one genuinely know oneself? The Bible's answer to that is, no, one cannot know themselves. Paul even went so far as to say, "No one can judge my motivations. I cannot even judge myself." For the conscience to find rest, it takes more than behavior modification and sin management. It takes something that reaches the innermost being so that gives a sense of righteousness, i.e. perfection, beyond mere action. It takes the blood of Jesus going into the Holy of Holies of who we are. For it is the only thing the conscience will accept if it is going to shut it down in terms of demand and accusation.

The conscience is a demanding drill sergeant, screaming orders and making demands. It reminds us of what we should be and yet are not. On the other hand, if the conscience is a sort of drill sergeant, than the flesh is more along the lines of a patronizing mistress. As opposed to the conscience's appeal to what is ideal, the flesh appeals to your basic survival and existence. It relates to you not in the arena of what you should be but rather in the arena of what you really are. The flesh doesn't scream for you to get your act together. It whispers that you deserve more. It offers excuses to indulge it and reminds you that it ("it" being you) is not appreciated enough. The Enemy works through both the conscience and the flesh. He uses the conscience to accuse and condemn you and he works through the flesh to tempt and seduce you. In other words, he will whisper through the mistress of temptation in order to then shout by way of the drill sergeant of condemnation. Keep in mind, his very name, "Devil", means Accuser. His primary goal is to make you feel shame, through condemnation, knowing that is how we are ground back down into the dust from which we came. He uses temptation as the means to condemnation, as he did in the Garden of Eden. If the devil can get you to sin through temptation, he then has means to bring shame through condemnation. That is why he both hisses as a serpent and then roars as a lion. He will hiss in patronizing tones for you to indulge the flesh, only to turn around and roar that you are a sinner. He will make it clear in which way you have missed the mark, right on the heels of showing you how you have every right to give in to the flesh. Christ declares that you have no rights and then reveal that you are no longer a sinner when you accept this. Satan will declare that you have every right and then reveal that you are a sinner because you gave in. Sin leads to death because of such condemnation. A guilty conscience sets into motion a domino effect that brings forth personality disorders, neurotic behavior, hostile attitudes, and over narcissism. These are the results of a messed up conscience, one that is shouting and demanding. Depression, chronic illness, and physical symptoms all can be triggered by a conscience that will never shut it down. The answer to these symptoms of a sin consciousness is coming to the Table of the Lord and finding rest.

The Table of The Lord speaks to the conscience within us and says, "It is Finished". It addresses the drill sergeant within by declaring "It is perfect". And that shuts down condemnation. It turns to the mistress and speaks, "My grace is enough". That shuts down temptation. In both condemnation and temptation, the root issue is "not enough-ness". But the Finished work of the Cross demonstrates that you do not need to do more or have more to be righteous. You cannot be any more complete than you are at this moment in the Finished work of the Cross.

"It is Finished" wins the war against our Enemy. It shuts down the drill sergeant and the mistress with equal severity. We destroy our enemy's ability to tempt and accuse when we take Communion. I wonder if we too often assume we come to the

Lord's Table after we have defeated our enemy rather than when we are being defeated. We buy into his lies if we believe we can come boldly to the Lord's Table once we have our act together. That is the exact opposite of how God's grace works. How foolish to say to an ill person that first they must overcome their disease before they go to the hospital or see a doctor. No! Jesus said it is not the healthy that need a physician but the ill and the weak. He said He did not come for the righteous ones who have defeated their enemies, but for the unrighteous who are still warring against their enemies. The Lord's Table is prepared, the Body and the Blood set out, right in the middle of the battle with our sins and demons. Even as we stumble, we do so in the direction of the Lord's Table. It is when we are at our weakest that we find the Body and Blood to be the strongest.

It was at the table that Esther defeated her enemy. Satan himself sat at the table with Jesus and The Twelve when he entered Judas. In both instances, the enemy was destroyed at the table. We come to the table to defeat our enemies, not because they are disposed of. We do not overcome them and *then* come to the Table; we overcome them as we bring them to the Table. I am thrilled that the Good Shepherd doesn't set the Table up after I've quieted my conscience and had victory over my flesh, but that He sets it up as the flesh is pulling and the conscience is demanding. A Table set up in the "presence of my enemies."

When the conscience demands, "Do more," and the flesh whispers, "Need more," it is the shout from the Cross that drowns them out with, "It is Finished!" No place is this shout declared with more clarity than at the Table of the Lord. Just as the High Priest made his way through the Outer Court, and through the Inner Court, then sprinkled the blood in the Holy of Holies. When we take communion, the Blood of Jesus is sprinkled beyond our consciousness and even beyond our conscience. It goes into our very subconscious. All that which transpires "behind the veil" of what we even know about ourselves is also being covered by the power of the Blood of Jesus. This is why healing takes place on so many levels. The power of condemnation is being broken in the deepest places and darkest shadows of our being.

To the Church in Corinth, Paul's admonition to them was to "examine themselves" when they came to the Lord's Table. This is the one place in the New Testament we are told to place any kind of focus on ourselves in terms of examination. The context of such instruction was that they needed to determine whether or not each of them was taking the Lord's Table seriously. Some were behaving as though they were not. People were getting drunk off the wine and others were hoarding the bread. As a result, Paul states that many were sick and dying. They missed out on the healing power of Communion because they were not taking the Finished work of the Cross and appropriating it deeply enough. The Lord's Table should be taken as seriously as possible but in this regard: the more seriously one takes the Finished work of the Cross, the less seriously one will take one's self. In other words, if I take the Table of the Lord seriously, it will cause me to relax. Interestingly, in the Old Testament, the same Hebrew word for "healing" is also used for the word "relax." The stripes of Jesus bring forth healing because He did all the work which precipitates rest for my soul. My soul gives rest to my body and a body at rest is a body that will heal. During His Earthly ministry, Jesus healed more people on the Sabbath Day than any other, as recorded in the Gospels. This demonstrates how important resting in the Finished work of the Cross is to the process of healing both mind and body.

I suggest that the more I relax through the Finished work of the Cross, the stronger my body will get and the quicker it will recover from my illness. I believe that my auto-immune disease, where the body will not shut down the immune system and, thus, attacks itself; will continue to abate as my conscience is daily being told of just how finished the Finished work of the Cross truly is.

The Finished Work of the Cross making its way into your conscience is like turning on a light switch. You may not know the intricacies of electricity. You may not be able to explain all the laws, not to mention or even know what they all are. For most of us, it is best we leave the electrical wiring in a building project to the experts because we have no idea how it all works. But when it comes to actually turning on the lights in a room, you don't need to know any of those things to make them work for you. Even my kids when they were two years old had the same capability as a NASA engineer when it came to flipping on a light switch to turn on the lights. As with a current of electricity, the current of God's Spirit, one that Paul calls the "The Spirit of Newness of Life," flows into your conscience and subconscious. You might not know how all the "wiring" works or the laws operate, but when you take the Lord's Supper or contemplate the Finished work of the Cross, all the spiritual power of that reality activates and sets into motion within you.

The Lord's Table defeats the Enemy by overcoming his accusations. The Book of Revelation tells us that the Accuser is overcome through two things: the Blood of the Lamb and the testimony of the Saints. The blood and our story go hand-in-hand to overcome the Devil. As mentioned, his name means

"Accuser", with the emphasis on the action of slander. He operates in the arena of shame. And when we choose to share our personal story of how God's grace has overcome our sin, it flies directly in the face of the Devil's entire program and stifles his mission. For if he can shame us into keeping our stories to ourselves, then he will have succeeded. What defeats the Devil is when we share our story with no shame because at the center of the story is the Blood.

I believe that too often we attribute the condemnation of the devil to the work of the Holy Spirit. The Holy Spirit will never condemn a believer in Jesus Christ. However, I have seen too many Christians, myself included, who assume that the feeling condemnation over their sin is from the Spirit. They mistake conviction with condemnation. Peter tells us that the Devil prowls *like* a roaring lion. He is not a lion but masquerades as one. To put it in Disney dialect, the Devil is the Scar to Jesus' Mufassa. Jesus is the genuine Lion of the Tribe of Judah. The Devil seeks to impersonate Jesus by being "like" a lion. He wants you to think that the Lord is frustrated with you. He roars, wanting you to believe God is a Drill Sergeant rather than a Good Shepherd. Conviction can be helpful in causing us to grow and improve through repentance, but shame is of no help whatsoever. In fact, shame destroys.

Where conviction deals with what you do, shame pertains to who you are. So when the Devil is accusing you, it will go beyond your mere action and down into the questioning and accusing of your very being. Surely the Spirit of the Lord lovingly speaks to us about what we do. After all, this is called Wisdom and Wisdom is a Woman that cries out in the streets. But when you begin to feel condemned over who you are, that is not the work of the Spirit in the heart of the Believer. It is the

Accuser. I believe, all too often, when we feel heavy or condemned over who we are, we wrongly say something to the effect of, "Help me, Lord, for I am wrong", when that wasn't the work of the Spirit at all. In fact, it comes from the Devil. The way you overcome this kind of shame is through the Blood and your testimony.

Healing is given and victory granted at the Table of the Lord because we are not focused on those sins and issues that have, in fact, been dealt with through the Finished work of the Cross. The attention is not on our sin but rather that our sin is forgiven. One of the core principles of the New Covenant is that God says, "I will remember your sins no more." Unlike the Old Covenant, in which unending sacrifices had to be made, the sacrifice of Jesus was once-and-for-all. I imagine the priests must have often sighed at the site of the sinner walking into the Courtyard yet again, with the sin offering standing by the sinner's side. The priest knew it would be a lot of work and may have thought, "Here we go again." However, the Finished work of the Cross is so complete and the offering Jesus made is so perfect, that when you or I sin, God will never roll His eyes and sigh, saying, "Here we go again." In fact, we might be frustrated with ourselves and say to God, in the illustrious words of Britney Spears, "Oops, I did it again." And we cry out of despair to God, "I blew it again. I messed up again. I sinned again!" And God says to us in moments like that, "Again?" He has chosen to limit Himself when it comes to recollection of our sin. He is not focused on our sin, He sees us in our Savior.

There was a breakthrough I had at Communion not too long ago. The Lord spoke to my heart and said, "Peter-John, if I don't remember your sin then neither should you." The power of Communion and the Finished work of the Cross is that it allows us not only to know God has forgiven us but also to be able to forgive ourselves. Although we have an Accuser who takes inventory of our sins with meticulous detail and drags them back to the attention of conscience, we have a Savior Whose grace is much greater than our sin. When the Accuser comes to the Judge of us all with thick files full of our sins and mistakes, God says to him, "I have no idea what you are talking about." Case dismissed!

Rest Stop 2: The Sea of Galilee

Jesus prepared breakfast for His disciples by the shores of the Sea of Galilee. It was a meal consisting of fish and it was for fishermen. They had spent the entire night before searching for the very thing that Jesus had cooking over some coals, and when they made it to the shore, it was ready and waiting. That little vignette from the Gospel of John has the same element of "finished-ness" to its narrative that the Table of the Lord and the Garden of Eden have in theirs. For while that fishing endeavor of the disciples was fruitless and they had come up with nothing in their own effort, Jesus had waiting for them what they had been searching for all along. He invited them to come and join Him and enjoy what He had done for them. A beautiful picture of the Finished work of the Cross.

Galilee is one of the world's best kept secrets despite the fact no other region has been more read and talked about the past two thousand years. To this day, it remains rural and underdeveloped even though the climate is ideal and the topography is gorgeous. It is a natural destination point for tourism and yet there is a conspicuous absence of high rise hotels and luxury resorts. There are no fortune five hundred companies located there, nor towering skylines of commerce. I believe that this is Divinely planned. For God has preserved the natural ambiance of Galilee so the pilgrim that travels there can still get a feel for what it was like when Jesus grew up and lived in that region. Once there, it doesn't take more than a day or so to recognize why Jesus would choose to base His public ministry from Galilee rather than Jerusalem. Just as in Jesus' time, Jerusalem exudes a cultural tension and political edge while Galilee is peaceful to the point of being characterized as sleepy. It was in the off the map towns and roads in the northern region of Israel that Jesus took the time to teach His disciples what it meant to work out of rest.

"Come and eat" was the invitation Jesus gave to His disciples in John's last chapter. This was not the first time Jesus enjoyed a meal with His friends after He had risen from the dead. While the dust was yet settling upon the first sightings of the living Jesus, He walked the Emmaus Road and ate with two unsuspecting followers of His. Upon appearing to The Twelve for the first time upon His resurrection, Jesus asked them, "Do you have anything to eat?" And here He is sharing food as well as conversation with them yet again. Think of the joy it brings Jesus each time you and I eat with Him! He says, "I knock on the door. Anyone who will let me in, I will come and eat with them." Notice that Jesus extends the invitation to invite Him. He extends that invitation to anyone who will open the door. He just so loves to eat because it is the place of shared communion Jesus desires with us. Only one place in the life of Jesus did He tell someone to "hurry up." It was when He told Zacchaeus, the tax collector, to hurry down from the fig tree that he was perched up in. What was so pressing as to warrant this imperative? Jesus was in a hurry to eat with Zacchaeus. I'll bet Jesus knowing that Zacchaeus was a man of means, as well as a sinner, knew how to throw a genuine party and one that would have some good food! Just as with Zacchaeus, Jesus is excited to eat with you.

Back to the breakfast by the sea, Peter had been joined by a few other disciples on that futile fishing expedition. It had been three years before, on that same seashore, that Jesus had called Peter, James, and John to follow Him and become "fishers of people. " Without hesitation, they abandoned their fishing business, boats and all, to follow the Lord. Now, after encountering Jesus following His death and resurrection, the fishermen returned to their fishing boats. Here they were again, following three years of teaching, miracles, and conversation with Jesus. They had come full circle. Maybe they were back on their boat because they were simply doing what men have done in similar circumstances of uncertainty both long before and after this story played out. When all else fails, or at least gets stressful, grab the fishing pole and get away from it all. Perhaps, then, things will work themselves out and the problem will be solved by the time the fisherman comes home. But I have a hunch it was something more than just decompressing that caused Peter and his fishing buddies to go back to their former lifestyle once again.

I think they didn't believe that Jesus needed them any longer. They had failed Jesus miserably when He needed them the most, in the hour that they could have proved their fidelity and love to Him, all they proved was how unreliable they were. Not only had they abandoned Jesus when He was being arrested in the Garden but even when He had risen, Jesus found them locked away in a room and hiding. He found them in a place of not taking the torch and carrying on the ministry of the Kingdom. It was if they had been caught in the act of failure. Indeed, they rejoiced when they saw Jesus was alive. After all, He was their Friend and their Rabbi. They would know He was the undeniable Savior of the World because He was alive. And not only that, His resurrection meant that everything between Jesus and them had not ended on the terrible note that they assumed it had. These disciples not only knew the Gospel, they were front and center in watching it transpire. However, none of that changed the fact that while Jesus had succeeded, they had failed. To them, "It is Finished" meant that Jesus had accomplished it all and there was nothing left for anyone to do.

At least, not for *them*... Why would there be? They had their chance and they blew it. So they went back to the fishing boats they had left three years previously. Then, just as He had done before, Jesus calls them though they felt unneeded. And that was the very reason He did so.

I believe most Christians do not fulfill the Great Commission out of apathy. There is that to some degree. In my observation, I have the greater dilemma in our sharing the Good News is that we feel as though we are not good enough. It is not for a lack of motivation but qualification that keeps our mouths shut. But then there are the coals. I think of the prophet Isaiah, a man who felt the same sense of ineptitude as a preacher of God's Word as the disciples did a thousand years later. As Isaiah is standing in the presence of God in a vision he had, He stated, "I am falling apart for I am a man of unclean lips." Isaiah evidently had a speech problem is the implication. Maybe it was habitually swearing or perhaps it was slander. In either case, he felt completely unqualified to be the prophet God was calling him to be. Just then, an angel took a coal from the altar and touched it to Isaiah's lips. God asked, "Who will go for Us." The man who just had stated his unworthiness answered, "Here I am" to the call. It was the coal to his lips that allowed him to go and preach what many call the "Fifth Gospel." The coal off of the altar speaks to a total and complete sacrifice. For us, it pertains to the Finished work of the Cross. And just as Isaiah and Peter felt unqualified to preach the Good News because they were not good enough, you and I might hesitate to preach the Gospel of the Finished work of the Cross for the same reason. But it was by the coal from the altar that allowed Isaiah to carry on. And it was by the coals of the fire that Jesus would tell Peter to feed His sheep.

The conclusion I come to when reading Jesus' conversation with Peter, one shared over fish and coals, was that not only did Jesus love Peter more than Peter loved Jesus but that was exactly the point of the conversation. Three times Jesus asked Peter to affirm his love for Jesus and in each of those requests Peter failed to respond in a love that was proportionate to Jesus' for him. Jesus told Peter that He loved him and Peter told Jesus that he liked him. And Jesus accepted that. He didn't sideline Peter and place him on leave of absence until the level of love could be reciprocated. Each of those lackluster responses garnered a fresh commission for Peter to feed the sheep. Yet not only was it established that Jesus loved Peter more than the other way around, and not only was Jesus demonstrating that was okay, I believe that Jesus wanted that to be established as the basis for Peter's commission to feed the flock of God. It would be Peter's understanding that his love for Jesus was inferior to Jesus' love for him that would serve as the prime motivation for Peter's ministry and life from that day forward. Jesus was saying that because Peter did not love Him as much as He loved Peter that now it was time to preach the Gospel and carry on the mission. This is incredible to me as a preacher, myself. I see it work every time. That is, the reverse psychology of grace. When I am stupefied and amazed at Jesus' love for me, it is then I preach with passion and serve with freedom. It is when I recognize that my love and devotion are never going to rise to the level of Jesus' love and devotion for me that I find myself "accidentally" loving Jesus more than I ever had before. I am impressed at the genius of Jesus' charge to Peter, as well as you and I, that it is because we will never love Him as much as He loves us that we must share His love with one another and this Good News to the whole world.

Peter would become a pastor knowing that he would never love Jesus as much as Jesus loved him. He carried this in his heart up to the moment he died. We know this because history states that Peter was crucified in Rome and he was crucified upside down. This was at his own request because he did not feel worthy to die in the same posture as His Lord. Peter knew Jesus loved him, a love of which he never had seen before or would since. And this caused him to share the Gospel with the Gentiles before anyone else had. For Peter knew what it meant to be saved by Grace and not Law. He preached with boldness even when imprisoned and beaten. This was because he could risk looking like a fool knowing He was affirmed by the One who mattered most. He healed the sick and raised the dead. For he made it clear that "it was not by our own power and righteousness that this man who was lame is now standing in front of you." Peter was restored by the Sea of Galilee because he finally understood that it was Jesus who loved him more than he loved Jesus and that would be the power that would flow from his life.

Jesus blessed the disciples with an enormous catch that morning even though they were not where they probably should have been. Whatever their intentions were, the fact that the disciples were out fishing just after history had been completely altered by their Lord speaks to the condition of their hearts. They certainly were not out fishing to do the work of the Kingdom. They did not go there in anticipation of meeting Jesus. And yet, there was Jesus; standing by and waiting for them to finally be so exhausted from their little expedition that they would come to shore. As the sun began to rise, Jesus shouted over the waters, "Kids, did you catch any fish." Not yet recognizing it was Him, they replied with a terse, "No." Things were so bad they couldn't even respond with the proverbial,

"...you should have seen the one that got away" retort. It was then Jesus told them, "Try the right side." He says the same to us when we are exhausted in our own efforts to fish out success and haul in righteousness. The "right side" in the Bible is always the position of righteousness. It is at the right hand of God the Father that Jesus is now seated. The prophet Isaiah states that God says He holds us up by the "right hand of My righteousness." So when we are tired from our futile fishing expeditions, the Lord also says to us, "Try the right side". The right side is resting in the Finished work of the Cross. Fishing from any other part of the boat is a waste of time.

The catch was so enormous that John was able to connect the dots and recognize just Whom it was that had given the order to toss their nets on the right side. As the boat began to sink from the haul of fish, John exclaimed, "It's the Lord!" Notice, He didn't merely say, "It is Jesus." He gives authority to Jesus and his submission is seen in that statement. Like the disciples, Jesus will bless us when we do not deserve it because we have no choice but to say, "It's the Lord." By that, I mean: First, we give Him all the credit, as do the people around us who observe the unmerited favor and blessing in our lives. I won't say, "It's Pete" when I realize how amazing God's grace has been to me. Second, it is His kindness that causes us to submit to His authority in our lives. God blesses us when we least deserve it because that is what brings about repentance. It is grace that changes hearts and that grace means our boats are filled and overflowing when we least deserve it.

I see this whole scenario that John writes about as rich in metaphor. For example, he specifically writes that upon catching the fish in the sea, the disciples' "net did not break." We might wonder why John would record that. Yet keep in mind, this entire narrative of the breakfast by the sea was written following the resurrection of Jesus. So all of it is alluding to various aspects of the Finished work of the Cross. Regarding the nets not breaking, it was three years before that Jesus had given Peter the same command to throw his nets to the right side of the boat. Just as in this account, when Peter did what Jesus had said, the catch was too big for his boat and it began to sink. Not only that, Luke records that the nets broke. The catch was made and the fish were there but Peter and the disciples could not keep what they had caught. The blessing had been there all along they just did not have the ability to receive it. Before we experienced the Finished work of the Cross, the blessings and promises of God were there, ready and available, yet we couldn't receive them. No matter how much effort we made to "haul them in" it was never enough. When striving in my own effort to merit the blessings of "the right side", i.e. righteousness, I take on the mindset of "not enough". I pray but I did not pray long enough. I spend time with my kids but not enough time. I earn a salary but it is not big enough. And on and on it goes. The net breaks and our souls are like sieves, not able to find the rest that comes with the contentment that comes through knowing what is "enough". It is the Finished work of the Cross, the call Jesus made to throw the nets on the right side after the resurrection as opposed to the call He made before it, that finally allows me to receive the blessings of the Lord. The Finished work of the Cross is the net that does not break.

Rest Stop 3: The Garden of Eden

Paradise is working out of perfection rather than working for it. I often try to remind my teenagers that work was not a result of the curse! The result of the curse was the stress that comes from work. And the reason there is any stress related to work is that when one is working in order to justify oneself rather than working out of the sheer pleasure of the work in itself. In other words, the Garden of Eden was paradise because Adam and Eve worked out of something that was already perfect. The work they did in the Garden was out of the sheer joy of the work they were doing. Like them, we will find our office environment, our field of vocation, our calling at home, and our ministry in the Church to be a labor of love rather than one of obligation when we recognize the work for our righteousness is already finished. We now are able to work out of that.

"Your problem is that you try too hard." Those were the words spoken to me by my friend in St. Louis, Missouri. Upon saying "I do", my wife and I packed up our wedding gifts and moved to the Midwest to plant a church. Without knowing a single person when we got there, after two years the church we planted had grown to about one hundred and fifty people. However, we were exhausted. My wife had already suffered a miscarriage and I was recovering from a brutal surgery. At the same time I was recovering, our first daughter, Bailey, was born to us. We decided it was time for us to move back to the Northwest and get our feet back under us again. I called the leaders of the church together to tell them I would be going and another man would be coming to pastor. It was during that meeting, my friend, older than I, had tears welling up in his eyes and told me that my problem was that I was trying too hard. Seventeen years, four children, three churches, two surgeries, and one bruised ego later, I look back and see how right his words were. My Crohn's Disease has allowed, no, forced me not to "try too hard." In fact, through my illness I have found that the secret to life is just that, resting in the Finished work of the Cross. Just as Yoda had wisely told young Luke Skywalker, "You do or do not. There is no try," my friend's advice not to try too hard falls very much under the principle of resting in the Finished work of the Cross. Through "it is finished", we do not try to be righteous or justified. We rest in the fact that we already are.

On the seventh day, God rested. We read of no eighth day. It means that Sabbath was perpetual in the Garden of Eden. So Adam and Eve worked on the Sabbath. Jesus would heal on the Sabbath. Then, He would rise on the Sabbath. This is all to demonstrate that the point of Sabbath is that it is all rest and not work. It means that we work out of rest! In the Garden, everything was taken care of and yet Adam and Eve still had plenty to do. The Garden watered itself but they still tended it. The animals came to Adam and he defined them. It was when Adam rested that Eve was brought to him. It was all a labor but it was a labor of love.

Paradise is simultaneously working and resting. Jesus offers us a yoke in connection with giving rest for our souls. He is inviting us back to Eden, which is to work out of the work that is finished. Sabbath a day, it's a condition of the soul and a way of life. It's a state of being whether on the job or on vacation.

The more secure I am in the Finished work of the Cross, the more genuinely I am inspired to want to serve God and others. This is why it is called the "fruit of the Spirit" as opposed to the "works of the Spirit". When we are living, loving, and serving out of the Finished work of the Cross, it is not on the basis of increasing our effort. In fact, I daresay, it becomes less effort; something that is "effort-less." Working out of rest allows me to go with the flow rather than my making it happen, In sports, a common refrain amongst coaches and teachers is for athletes to "let the game come to you." In forcing the action, the player is much more prone to errors on the playing field; such as dropping the pass or dribbling the ball off the foot. But if one is relaxed and going with the flow, you are actually able to do much better than if you were overly intense and wound way too tight. In the Garden, Adam and Eve were able to "let the game come to them".

To take Jesus' yoke and His burden means we don't strive to do good works, but we flow in them. On the day we stand before God, Jesus states that those who have trusted in Him will say, "When did we feed you and visit you in prison?' And I will say to them, 'When you did it to the least of them you did it for Me." Those who trust their righteousness to the Finished work of the Cross are not even conscious of the good things that they do. Conversely, Jesus said those who are not righteous will say to Him on That Day, "'Lord, Lord, we did many mighty things in your name, we prophesied and cast out demons.' And I will say, 'I don't know what you are talking about, and I do not know you'" Those who seek to make their own case through their performance are so aware of the good works they have accumulated and are so focused on taking inventory of them that they are not even credited with them. The reason is that these so called "good works" are, in fact, full of hidden agendas and ulterior motives. Perhaps they do these works in order to compensate for other flawed areas of their lives. But one thing for certain, they all fall under the category of "dead works" according to the New Testament.

Eden is characterized by fruit. The work of the flesh comes as a result of not believing the work is already finished. The fruit of the Spirit blossoms through this realization: I am just as righteous before God, and thus worthy of his love and blessing, when I am not doing good things as when I am, because it is based on what Jesus has done and has zero to do with what I have done. This is essential to bearing more fruit. The Garden of Eden is watered by the Finished work of the Cross.

I believe that part of the reason Abraham and Sarah were finally able to have a child in their very old age was that they stopped trying too hard. Sometimes it is when circumstances seem so impossible and we give up on them that grace comes in, if only to show us that it is not about us. It is common knowledge that if a woman is extremely focused on having a child it actually lessens her chances. The more stress a person in under, the less their body has the natural ability to reproduce. Have you ever heard a couple declare that they are trying to have a baby? First of all, that is too much information. But more than that, they are putting so much stress on themselves through focusing on having a child that it could possibly hinder the process. Seriously, it is when a couple is not trying to have a baby that, all too often, that is when one comes!

For years, Abraham and Sarah were "trying" to have a baby. They even went the surrogate-mistress-route, and we still see the mess that created to this day. The name of the son born to them was Laughter. Each of them laughed when they were told that they would have a baby. Like Abraham, we don't laugh at God when we rest in the Finished work of the Cross, but we can laugh with Him in amazement of His grace. The more seriously we take the Finished work of the Cross, the less seriously we take ourselves. And the less seriously we take ourselves the more we are able to see "Isaacs", that is fruit, produced in our lives. The statement that "God helps those who help themselves" could not be more counterproductive to bearing fruit in our lives. In fact, God helps those who cannot help themselves. And what's more, God helps those who will not help themselves.

Sabbath means "Stop." When I am overly focused on what I need to be doing rather than what Jesus has already done, I need to Sabbath it right then and there. To "be still and know that He is God". I need to "stand still and see the work of God" and to see that "the battle is not yours but the battle is the Lord's." I need to stop digging lest the hole I am in only gets deeper. The best way out of the hole is to rest in His grace.

The Garden of Eden was full of fruitful trees that were productive on restful Sabbath. One comes as a result of the other. The less I try, the more fruitful I become. The rest in the Sabbath actually causes us to do more than the demands of the Law. Jesus said that the greatest man who ever lived was John the Baptist. Yet John never did a single miracle in his entire life. What John did do was point people to Jesus, and his lasting legacy was in this statement made after he died: "All the people said that 'John did no mighty miracle but the things he said of Jesus were true." When the scribes and the Pharisees came to John, questioning his authority, they asked him who he was. The first thing he said in response to that question was who he wasn't. "I am not the Christ".

When I was in my late teens, I was doing what many at that age do: sorting out my identity and trying to figure out what the trajectory of my life might be. In a time of frustration, I told my dad, "I don't even know what I am." He said to me, "I can tell you who you are not." We both knew he was referring to John's statement about not being the Christ. Looking back I see the fatherly wisdom of not being overly focused on who I am but rather, like John, emphasize in my life and thoughts, who Jesus is.

The Bible is not a story about good guys and bad guys, so try and be one of the good guys. The story of the Bible reveals that even the good guys are bad guys. If you think your family is dysfunctional, read the stories of the Patriarchs: Abraham, Isaac, and Jacob. Those stories will make you feel better about your situation in no time. Talk about the "Real Housewives of the Promised Land." My point is that the Bible is a story about one "Good Guy" who doesn't take bad people and make them good so much as take dead people and make them alive. The doctrine of Justification is that of God taking wrong people and making them right. John simply being aware of Jesus' person in relationship to his was what made John the greatest man ever. Then Jesus said something even more astounding than that. He said that the person who is the least in the Kingdom of God is greater than John the Baptist. What this means is that the person who is least and does the least under the New Covenant is greater than the person who is the most and does the most under the Old Covenant. What makes this so? Because even the "worst" person under the New Covenant is made righteous through the work of Jesus and not their own. Elijah raising the dead or Moses parting the Red Sea cannot even make it into the same arena as the perfect work of the Cross! You are greater in the Finished work of the Cross than any person who has done work in their own effort and for their own righteousness. It is the finished-ness of the Cross that we rest in and the perfection of the Cross in which we boast. The beauty of Eden in its constant completion shows us that we are saved by Grace and that results in fruitfulness that no self effort could ever produce.

I amazed at how lifeless the trees that line the Rogue River look for eight months out of the year. If one didn't know better, the leafless branches and fruitless vines would seem to indicate that no life was present. Yet because fruit is not seen at the moment is not a definitive statement that the trees are dead. They are very much alive, even if there is no fruit. For in those winter months of fruitlessness, they are resting by the current of water and drawing nutrients in store for the season of fruitfulness that is to come. Just because I might be going through a barren, wilderness-like experience does not mean I am spiritually dead. As the tree in Psalm 1, I am simply to rest by the river of God's supply and drink it in anticipation of the season of fruitfulness that will surely come as a result of my resting.

The Psalmist gives us much hope when he states that the tree planted by the river will bring forth fruit "in its season." By virtue of the fact there are seasons, it means that I will not always be as "fruitful" during one period of my life as another. But here is the kicker: That is not the gauge of my right standing with Jesus as far as my level of righteousness is concerned! My fruitfulness, or lack thereof, does not determine if I am qualified for salvation. Neither does it merit my being blessed by God. For the blessings in my life, just as salvation, is contingent upon my faith in the fruitfulness of Jesus, not mine! The same way I was born again is also the same way that I bear fruit. And that is also the same way that I am blessed, filled with the Spirit, and made more and more like Jesus. It is by grace and grace alone!

Remember in the parable of the Prodigal Son, Jesus told us that upon his return to his father's house, the rebellious son received a coat, a ring, and a pair of sandals by his father. All three of those things indicated to the son and those who were connected to the family that there was work to be done. And that there was work to be done by the homebound son. The robe spoke of his identity and that he would represent his father. The rink pertained to authority and that he had the power to purchase. The shoes revealed his liberty. For slaves were not allowed sandals for the fear that they might run away. In each of those items, it revealed the son had not dropped to a place of insignificance in his family estate due to his departure. In fact, just the opposite, it seems as though he was given a position of favor and authority, one even higher than he had before he left. With people, if we walk away or disappoint them, it may be quite awhile before we work our way back to the place of trust or partnership that we had with them before. But with our Father, when we choose to come back to Him, it is as though we never left. He sees us no less or diminished upon our return home. And like the Prodigal, the Father says to us that we didn't earn that love and never will, and it is because of that we have a lot of work to do!

God sees me as having done every good work required for righteousness, even when I haven't. In fact, even though I haven't. I am counted as having done them through the Finished work of the Cross. I may not be as kind as I would like to be but I am counted as kind. I may not be patient but I am counted as though I am patient. This understanding brings me back to Eden because now I want to be kind and patient out of the sheer pleasure it gives me. It has been rightly said that we become what we already are. And rest for the soul brings greater works in this life.

In Luke 10, Martha was hosting Jesus and His disciples in her house. Her sister, Mary, was seated at Jesus' feet, which was the posture of a disciple. Martha called her out, saying to Jesus, "Lord, tell my sister to help me." Jesus quickly point out that to Martha that what her sister was doing, which was resting, was more important that what Martha was doing. Jesus told Martha that Mary had "chosen the better part". If there comes the choice of time allotted to serving the Lord or enjoying the Lord, Jesus wants us to choose to enjoy Him every time! We may wonder if it is actually beneficial to sin in the church sanctuary and listen to the sermon preached or sing songs of worship. Could we not be busy doing the work of the Kingdom? After all, looking at poverty in world today shows that there is a lot of work to be done. In this instance of Martha and Mary, Jesus says there in nothing more beneficial to the work of the Kingdom being accomplished than by sitting, resting, and enjoying the fact that the work of the Kingdom has already been accomplished. For a great irony is to be found in this account. In the final week of Jesus' life, it was Mary that came to His feet again. This time, though, not to sit and rest, but to anoint and bless. She took costly spikenard, an ointment used for burial in those times, and poured it on Jesus' feet. Interestingly, that very oil was also used for healing scars that were incurred upon the skin. Jesus pointed out that she had done this "for my burial" a week before He had even died. She was able to do something that neither Martha nor any other of the disciples seemed to be capable of doing. She foresaw the events of Jesus life and therefore gave to Him to enjoy before His death something that was always used for someone after their death. Mary did not do everything. She was not obligated to do everything. And because Jesus' words to Martha, she was justified in not doing everything. What Mary did do, though, was the right thing. And she did the right thing at the right time. And her offering of spikenard oil indicates she knew of

Jesus' coming death and symbolizes to us what it means to do the right thing in light of the Finished work of the Cross.

Personally, I only have so much left in the tank. I am not able to do near what I once did, nor what I would like to do. I often feel I am on the reserve tank, if not on fumes. I cannot do everything in a world that seems to demand I do. Maybe you feel a bit of that same frustration. The beauty of grace is that we are not called, nor even supposed to do everything. But if we rest in Jesus' finished work of the Cross, we will do the right thing.

All of this is comes from a state of rest. And that rest is a result of innocence. In the Garden, Adam and Eve worked out of a naiveté of good and evil. They were not "trying" to be good. They just were as they worked out of rest. The Tree of the Knowledge of Good and Evil was not a bad tree. It was included with the rest of the creation when God declared over it, "It is good". The problem was that the Tree of the Knowledge of Good and Evil was not good for Adam and Eve. Their systems would overload upon consuming the fruit of it. They were never intended by God to have the knowledge of what was good and what was evil. Think about that! They were simply to have an existence in an environment where they were absolutely free just to be. It doesn't mean they were not obedient to God, but rather they simply were not aware whether they were or not. A beautiful innocence where shame and condemnation had not yet entered. A return to Eden is recapturing the innocence that was lost when Adam and Eve gained the knowledge of good and evil. A child like faith is nurtured within us each time we are focused on the Finished work of the Cross rather than our own works and behavior. This is the essence of the Tree that they tragically neglected, which

41

was the Tree of Life. What really makes us alive is not knowing what is good and evil and basing our righteousness on that but rather knowing that the work for our righteousness is complete.

I have yet to see any young child constantly analyzing their own behavior when it comes to their qualification for blessing. When birthday presents are bestowed, there is yet to be the child that bows to the earth and grovels, saying, "Mom and Dad, I am not worthy of such generosity." The kids know they are not perfect. They also know the gifts are not based on their perfection or lack thereof. They do not sit around the table all day and wonder if dinner will be on their plate that night. There is a righteous sense of entitlement that because they are our kids there will be dinner for them when the time comes. Jesus applauds that kind of innocence we see in our children. I wouldn't be happy if they felt any other way than "entitled" when it comes to being loved by their parents. When Jesus hung on the Cross and said to the thief, "Today, we will be in Paradise together", Jesus was speaking of this kind of relationship one has with God through the Cross. And for us, Paradise is found when we gain back that innocence we lost through the knowledge that we sin and instead grow in the knowledge that through Jesus' perfection, we too have been made perfect.

As dreadful the impact of Adam's sin has had on our lack of innocence, the work of Jesus is greater than Adam's failure. And the Finished work of the Cross is by far greater than loss of our innocence. What you or I have done in our past is not a match for Jesus' shout "It is Finished".

Rest Stop 4: The Ark of Noah

Noah prepared the Ark for others to step into and be saved. Ironically, the hardest working man in the Old Testament had a name that mean "Rest". God gave Noah an assignment that took nearly one hundred years to complete. Five times the Scripture account says that Noah "did all that God commanded him and finished the work". Five is the number of grace. The Ark is an enormous display of Finished work of the Cross in that it speaks to something prepared and complete, all the believer has to do is to get on board.

Just as Noah, Jesus finished all that God the Father had commissioned Him to do. This Divine Assignment give to Jesus was commenced when He was baptized in the Jordan River and a dove descended upon Him there. The comparison with Noah is easily drawn in Jesus' submersion that represented His submission to God. The Bible states that Baptism is pictured by the Flood of Noah's Day and the dove also descended upon Noah on the face of the waters. Like the Ark, the work of the Cross was a massive undertaking. It was meticulously planned and it was followed through to the last detail. As with the Ark, there was nothing left to be done in order to be shielded from God's justice.

Skeptics have wondered how a single vessel could possibly contain two of every kind of species of animals. It has been calculated for that to happen, the boat that Noah built would have to be equivalent to the size of thirty-three railroad box cars. According the measurements in the Bible, Noah's Ark had dimensions equal to over five hundred boxcars! There was more than enough room for all. And while under normative circumstances, differing species could never co-exist in an enclosed environment; somehow the floating habitat was able to keep them each secure. In the Finished work of the Cross, there are people from every kind of demographic and age group. Uniquely of all world religions, it is Christianity that has had a major impact on each habitable continent, including Antarctica! When Jesus said that in the Father's House there would be many mansions with many rooms, He meant it! There is enough room for all who look to the Cross as the means of righteousness. Scanning the faces of folks who make their way to the Lord's Table day by day, it is a credit to the all-encompassing and relevant Finished work of the Cross. Nothing could bring so many, from such different places; into a oneness of the like the world has never seen. There is a common denominator that supersedes any one political ideology, favorite sports team, or shared interests. It transcends race, culture, and language. It is a "boatful" of people that otherwise may have had little to nothing in common. However, the more diverse and eclectic a gathering of people, the more power to the cause and purpose of that gathering. The word "Church" means "called out". And in my opinion, what makes the party at the Father's House so exciting is that "prodigals" have made their way there from all kinds of places; even as different species and creatures made their way to the Ark of Noah. The Finished work of the Cross does truly cross every culture and continent and goes into the ends of the world to bring His children home.

The Ark Noah built was sealed "inside and outside", according the Scriptures. It was airtight and there was no possibility that the floodwaters could even begin to seep inside. The pitch that sealed the Ark is referred to as "kaphar" in the Hebrew language. It literally means "covering." What is interesting about "kaphar" is that is the word also used in Leviticus for the word "atonement". When people brought their animal sacrifices to the Tabernacle for their sins, what they received was "kaphar" or "atonement". This means that their sins were covered in the act of the sacrifice being offered on their behalf. One other place that the word "kaphar" is used in the Bible is in reference to the lid that sat on top of the Ark of the Covenant. The Mercy Seat, as it is called, is literally the word "kaphar" because it covers the stone tablets with the Ten Commandments etched upon them. The tablets were placed inside the Ark and were covered by the Mercy Seat. In both instances, the word "kaphar" shows how the people's failure to keep the Law and obtain righteousness through It were covered by God. This Atonement was what sealed the Ark that kept Noah, his family, and all creation safe inside. The Finished work of the Cross is what seals us from judgment and covers us from God's wrath. The Flood was indicative then, as His wrath is now, that God is settled in His opposition to evil. The same things that enrage us about injustice also enrages God. Even more so! He solved the cosmic dilemma of judging evil without destroy us through covering His people in the Ark of the Finished work of the Cross. Through the cry, "It is Finished!", Jesus was able to both demonstrate God's unwavering justice and, at the same time, justify us as sinners, making us righteous.

The Finished work of the Cross gives to us the covering we have been looking for since the Garden of Eden. We would have otherwise been in over our heads in the floods of our own unrighteousness had not God sent us One who built a prepared a righteousness that we simply stepped into by faith. As the Mercy Seat and the sacrifices of the Tabernacle accomplished, so the Finished work of the Cross is able to give us something by which we know that God has us covered. His justice has not been compromised in justifying us and, in fact, has been established in doing so. The Apostle John states that God is "faithful and just" in forgiving our sins. He is just to forgive us because Jesus paid our debt on the Cross. Therefore, as shocking as this sounds, God would be unjust if He hadn't forgiven us of our sins. That is how final and complete the work of Jesus is on our behalf. Jesus paid the debt. It would go contrary to God's justice to then make us pay it as well. Jesus served our sentence. It would not be just for God to judge us for sin that has already been judged. In the Rogue Valley, there are intentional "burn zones" for the purpose of keeping wildfires at bay. If an area has already been burned out, there is no possible way that fire can blaze through that area again. The Cross of Jesus was an eternal burn zone. That means, Jesus took the fire of God's indignation on our behalf so that we need not wonder if God is angry with us ever again.

Even as the Ark took the pounding from the elements of God's judgment so that those inside might do as Noah's name declared, which was "Rest", Jesus took the fullness of God's anger toward the evil, both what we have done, and that which has been done to us, and we rest under His covering. Every conceivable stage of anger that God might have demonstrated in His justice was fully absorbed by Jesus in our place. From the pounding of a fist to the rolling of the eyes, Jesus took that all away so that the only thing that remains when God sees you or I is His smile. The flood of righteous indignation has passed us over and we are now beneath the rainbow of God's favor and lovingkindness.

The Ark of our righteousness is airtight, sealed by the Blood of Jesus, and not even a drop of God's anger will seep through. There is no loophole in heaven or earth that the Devil might use to try and condemn us with. The Book of Hebrews tells us that at this very moment, Jesus is seated at the right hand of God

Himself and that Jesus' very presence is what makes intercession for you and I. The word "intercession" that Hebrews chapter seven employs literally means "to hit the mark". If you are familiar with the etymology of the word "sin", you may know that it was a medieval archery term, one that meant to "miss the mark". When we "miss the mark" in our lives or thoughts, Jesus "hits the mark" for us. And not just when He died two thousand years ago. Hebrews stats that he "ever lives" to make intercession on our behalf. That means He is "hitting the mark" for us even as you read this! Your righteousness is as secure as Jesus seating in the throne room of Heaven. When Noah and his family boarded the Ark, the Bible states that it was the Lord that shut the door behind them. When you got on board with the Finished work of the Cross and rested in It as the means for your righteousness, it was the Lord that sealed you and is now keeping you within it. If God opens doors, no one can shut them. When it comes to your righteousness, if God is the one that shut the door behind you, no one can pry it back open!

To remain safe from the judgment of God, all Noah and the inhabitants of the Ark had to do was rest inside. The same was true when judgment passed over the land of Egypt in the time of the Exodus. The people of Israel were commanded to remain behind the door of which they had applied the blood of a lamb on that first Passover. Even as Atonement had sealed the Ark of Noah, it was Atonement that kept God's people from the judgment in Egypt. In both instances, it was not who the people were that preserved them from judgment but it was *where* they were that preserved them. The only thing that separated Noah from the outside judgment was the Ark and the only thing that identified the homes of the Children of Israel from that of the Egyptians was the blood. The rain came down and the Death

Angel passed over and all God's people had to do was remain in the place of rest. When it comes to the Finished work of the Cross, we simply need to remain and rest there. It does us no good and, in fact, is counterproductive to wander out and away from the place of simple and amazing grace as the basis of our righteousness. You never, ever move ahead and graduate from the grace that brought you into the Ark of God's righteousness. Stay in the house where the blood is applied. You need the Cross as much today as you did the day you were first saved. In fact, I believe that you and I need it more today than when we were born again.

Self-righteousness can become counterproductive because it sets us back through our own self effort. Resting in Christ's work for us moves us ahead if we remain in that place of trusting in the Finished work of the Cross, not only for salvation eternally but as the basis for blessing in our lives today.

Wisdom is found in a little chipmunk-like creature called the coney. The Book of Proverbs points to that little guy as an example of how to best leverage the environment around you to your advantage. The coney uses the strength of the rocks around it to hide because, in the words of Proverbs, the coney is a "feeble folk". Like the coney, we are feeble folk. The more we recognize this, the stronger we will be. For we are as strong as what we hide in to cover us. As Martin Luther stated, "We hide from God in God". There is no stronger place for us to rest and hide in than the Finished work of the Cross.

After the flood subsided, the Ark came to rest on a mountain called Ararat. The name Ararat literally means, "The Curse Reversed." It is not an accident that the place the Ark finally ended up in was called "Curse Reversed." Even those curses we have brought upon ourselves by sin and through our failures, when it comes to God guiding our lives and blessing our homes, He will turn it all around.

The Scripture says that the Ark rested on this mountain on the "seventeenth day of the seventh month." Scholars point out that according to the Jewish Calendar set up through Moses; the day would later become the day of the Feast of Firstfruits in Israel. Firstfruits was the feast that celebrated the beginning of the harvest three days following the Passover. That would be the day that Jesus rose from the grave. Paul would refer to Jesus as the "Firstfruits" of our resurrection. Consider just how "restful" the Ark was as it rested on the mountain. The man named "Rest" was in an Ark that was resting on a mountain of which had its foundation on the resurrection of Jesus. All our righteousness rests on the day that Jesus stepped out of the tomb. The Finished work of the Cross has at its foundation the glorious news that Jesus is risen. Jesus' rising from the dead is the sure validation that what we are resting in is worth investing our whole lives into. The evidence of Jesus' resurrection is such that *Newsweek* Magazine, not a periodical known for its Christian apologetics, begrudgingly admitted on its cover that something happened two thousand years ago which defies explanation. Where the critic looks to explain away the evidence, the Christian finds rest in it. Kenneth Laterrete, renowned Yale Historian, stated, "The more one examines the factors that seem to account for the extraordinary victory of Christianity, the more one is driven to search for a cause underlying them all. It is clear that the very beginning of Christianity, a vast release of energy was released, virtually unequalled in history, without it the future of the course of Christianity is unexplainable." When Jesus rose from the grave because we now rest in something that is on solid ground historically, as well as theologically.

49

Once the Ark was completed, everything flowed to it from its state of being finished. Just as in the Garden, we see how the animals came to Adam, the same principle of "letting the game come to you" is absolutely seen in Noah's Ark. The dove came to Noah when he was on the Ark. The dove is the symbol of the Holy Spirit. When you are resting in the Finished work of the Cross you are in the posture of rest through which you will be filled by the Spirit of God. In Galatians, Paul stated that the same way we receive the Holy Spirit is also the way we walk the Christian journey. What he is stating is that the filling of the Holy Spirit is not through motion and works but through rest and faith. God fills us when we are resting because you cannot fill a moving vessel. Not only did the Dove come to Noah but so did the animals. Like Adam in the Garden, Noah was given a mission pertaining to creation. And also like Adam, God brought the work to Noah. When we are at rest, we see success in our work because it comes to us rather that our striving to make it happen. Our disposition of peace will attract blessing and favor as it stands in stark contrast to the stress of the world around us. And finally, Noah's family followed him into the Ark. Whether it be family or friends, follow the Rest and the rest will follow.

The first thing you or I have to do for that to happen is to get on board for ourselves. Then those we love and are connected to will follow just as they did with Noah. If you are resting, they will also come into that place of rest. My dad pointed out in his commentary that Noah began the work of building the Ark for he, his wife, their sons, and their sons' wives, twenty years before his first son was even born. As Hebrews 12 specifically points out, the reason Noah built the Ark was in order to save his family. And therefore it was by faith he did so because his family wasn't even born yet! Like Noah, when we choose to rest in Finished work of the Cross, it will impact and entice others around us to do the same. The cumulative effect of daily Shalom that we live in will pave the way for our family, friends, and coworkers to follow. I wonder how much the peace and rest that Noah had during tumultuous days were able to attract the animals and creatures of nature the way it did. Was there a sort of Dr. Doolittle effect going on leading up to the Flood? Perhaps, yes. In any event, we need not debate or argue people into resting in the Finished work of the Cross. I have yet to see one person debated into the Kingdom of Heaven. What we can do is get on board ourselves and let the Spirit of the Lord do the rest.

By resting in the Finished work of the Cross, ironically you are building something for your family to come into and find blessing and peace. You are creating a covering for others to find rest. The rest that you have will attract those that follow you, as I am sure was the case with Noah. It all starts with you. You cannot change another person or calm their spirit. You can simply step into the Finished work of the Cross and be in that place of rest for yourself. Then from an overflow of peace will you be able to be a peacemaker. From a quiet spirit will you be able to quiet storms.

The key to getting our kids "on board" is not commanding them what they must do but reminding them what has been done for them. This is also true if you have employees or students. Any one of us that seeks to influence others in positive directions should employ the leadership model shown by Noah. Get on board first and then let the others follow. In this case, it means get on board in resting in the Finished work of the Cross for yourself. And emit to others the kind of attitude that is not demanding but rather supplying. That means moving away from the Law and into grace. Grace is something that will, ironically, have greater effectiveness than commandments. This is what Paul meant when he stated that the Law will bring death but the Spirit will bring life. At the core of the Law if the mantra, "Thou Shalt". The basis of the New Covenant, i.e. Grace, is "I will". When interjecting "thou shalt's" into a relationship and putting the onus of performance upon the other, it will eventually kill that relationship. Rather, when wanting to positively effect and direct another, the key is to give the person the assurance that you are there for them and avail what you have to them. Instead of demanding, when we are constantly offering, then eventually people tend to come around and get on board. This is ever true when it comes to seeing our friends and family "get on board" in believing the message of the Gospel. Constantly remind them not of what they should do but what has been done for them. And once you share the Good News with those whom you are waiting to get on board with you in the Finished work of the Cross, the most powerful thing you could ever do is to then rest.

We have considered the similarity of the Ark of Noah with that of the Ark of the Covenant being that of Atonement. However, there is also a great difference between the two as well. The difference is found in the very work "Ark." In the case of the Ark of the Covenant, the word "Ark" pertains to a coffin. In Genesis 50, where the Bible states that Joseph's bones were carried to Canaan in a coffin, the word used for "coffin" is also for "Ark" in the Ark of the Covenant. The Ark of the Covenant was a coffin, of sorts. For it was a box that carried within it the stone tablets that had etched upon them the Ten Commandments. The Law is so beautiful and holy that we cannot keep its standards for perfection and therefore if we seek righteousness through our performance in obeying it, the

Law brings death. However, it is buried and covered by the aforementioned Mercy Seat; the lid over it that speaks of Atonement. When it comes to the Ark that Noah built, on the other hand, the word does not pertain to a coffin at all. In 2 Chronicles, the Bible speaks about treasury boxes that were in the Courtyard of the Temple where people would deposit the money they had offered to God. The word that is used for those treasury boxes in the Temple is the same one used for Ark that Noah had built. Therefore, the Ark of Noah is described as being a treasure chest. Which makes whatever was inside the Treasure Chest of the Ark, nothing less than treasure. The Finished work of the Cross is a treasure chest. It was "preformed" by Jesus for the purpose of securing our righteousness and keeping you and I safe from judgment. It is indestructible and infallible. It cannot be broken or undone. And if that is the Treasure Chest, it makes any who are within the power of its framework nothing less than the Treasure! You are treasured by God. He has invested everything into you by giving His precious Son. And that gift not only obtained your righteousness but even right now it maintains it, as well. For God has placed you in the Finished work of the Cross in order to protect His investment.

There is a series on television called *Storage Wars* that is all about finding hidden treasure in abandoned storage units. People bid on the unit for auction without being able to go inside. They will purchase it based on a glance alone in hopes that buried inside of the cluttered mess is a something valuable enough to make the entire purchase worth the investment. When God sent His Son, it was a cosmic episode of *Storage Wars.* He purchased the entire world for the sake of extracting you! Jesus likened His mission to a man that stumbled upon a buried treasure in the field and was so thrilled that he sold everything he had to buy the entire field just for the treasure. In the Story of Ruth, the same kind of treasure hunt is romantically enacted when Boaz buys a neglected, foreclosed upon piece of property just for the opportunity of marrying Ruth. Redemption is such that God loved the whole world so that He gave His Son and yet, one is theologically on solid ground when we say that He bought the whole world just for you. Think it through, Jesus paid the price for "not only our sins but the sins of the whole world" in hopes that even if no one else in the world got on board through His sacrifice, even if you alone had done so it would have been worth the investment that He made and the price that He paid. All of that declares just how treasured you are!

Stay in the Treasure Chest. The storm is going to pass. Don't wander away from the Finished work of the Cross and lose your rest. Just as the storm subsided around Noah and the Angel of Death passed over the Children of Israel, if you are currently in the storm, wait it out! Just as it has become of God's judgment upon us, you will know the same truth will be of this present. And that truth is, "...and it came to pass."

Rest Stop 5: The Land of Canaan

As Eden was prepared for Adam and Eve, Canaan was prepared by God for the Children of Israel. Even as Noah and his family simply needed to get on board that which had been completed, the Children of Israel only needed to step into a land already conquered. All they had to do was take what was given. The reason they failed to do this was because they were focused on their own inability rather than God's ability. Too busy looking down at their own feet to step ahead. They were self conscious, and it crushed them.

The sure way to stunt your growth as a Christian is to focus on it. You will single inch to your physical stature by being worried about it, according to Jesus. The same is true in constantly evaluating your spiritual progress. When our kids brought home their first grade science project, a seed potted in a styrofoam cup, the lesson they learned was to leave the seed alone. If they would keep their fingers out of the soil, the seed would sprout on its own. If they thought they could check on the progress of the seed by unearthing it from the soil, they would discover that it would never grow at all. On many occasions, Jesus likened the Kingdom of God to a seed. It is something that takes place under the surface, working and producing fruit without our effort. IF we are constantly evaluating our performance and behavior as Christians, it will become counterproductive. The reverse psychology of grace is that the less you worry about your spiritual progress, the more spiritual progress there is to be had. When we want our kids to grow, we tell them to start trying harder. No, we understand it will happen on its own; naturally and organically and slowly. In fact, when we really want then to grow, we do the opposite of telling them to make a greater effort. Instead, we tell them to take a nap! When they are cranky and tired, the last thing they need to do is push through it. If necessary, we will make them go to bed against their will because we know that rest is the secret to growth.

The land of Canaan is referred to as *Rest* in the Book of Hebrews. Even as the Sabbath is more than a day it is a way of life, so the land of Canaan is more than a plot of territory: it is a condition of the soul. The land speaks to a state of being at rest. One that comes from the invitation that Jesus gives to find our soul's rest in Him. There is one time we are told to be afraid in the New Testament. It is in connection with the account of Israel's failure to conquer the Land of Canaan, and we are told we are to fear that we, likewise, fail to enter God's rest. The warning of the New Testament is not to be fearful we are not doing enough but to be fearful we are trying, in our own efforts, to do too much.

The people of Israel were so occupied with themselves they could not see beyond their own inadequacies and look at the Land as one that was all theirs for the taking. Ironically, it was in trusting their own strength which is what precipitated their backing down and walking away. The job of Israel was not so much to be victorious as believe that the victory was already accomplished. The promise that God had given them for the conquest of the land had nothing to do with their strength or ability. Yet they failed to expel the enemy from the land because they were focused on the proportion of their weakness to the strength of the occupants. "We are grasshoppers in our own eyes and in the eyes of the giants" was the report of the ten (apart from Joshua and Caleb). The Bible calls the testimony of the spies an "evil report". It wasn't simply negative news or tampered expectations, according to Scripture. It was a report that was "evil" because they took the attention and placed it squarely on their inability and shortcoming. When I hear "reports" coming from the pulpit that emphasize what people are failing to do as opposed to what God has done via the Finished work of the Cross, I recognize it for what it is. It's not Good News, rather, just the opposite. If you are hearing preached what you ought to be doing and yet are not, that might be news to you, but it is an evil report. Preaching the Law and not the Gospel is referred to as the "ministry of condemnation" by the Apostle Paul. It is one that leads to sin and brings death. The result of the evil report the spies brought forth paralyzed the people from moving ahead and making progress. The irony is that preaching the Law of Sin and Death is that showing people what they are not will only make them do less. The spies created a Grasshopper Complex in the minds of Israel. That is a mindset that people are not doing what they should and are, therefore, disqualified from inheriting the promises of God. What the spies (and subsequently) the people failed to remember is that the Land had already been given. It was prepared and ready; in other words, it was finished. Therefore, it had nothing to do with them at all. Thinking that it did was what ultimately kept them from taking the land.

As I stood in a line at Disneyland for ten hours (or so it seemed) to ride Indiana Jones, the message pounded into my head over the speaker was a warning not to look into the Evil Eye. IN the course of the adventure ride, there is an eye in the center of the ride, located in the ruins, that brings about a curse on anyone who looks into it. Evidently, someone in our car must have looked into the eye because our ride was stuck in the Temple of Doom. Sitting there amongst the ancient ruins, it got me thinking about, not eye problems, so much as "I" problems. That is how we curse our progress when we are focused on the

"I" rather than the Finished work of the Cross. We look to "I" rather than the "I AM" as the basis of whether or not we are qualified to take in the promises of God's Word. Grasshopper Complex sets in, as one is paralyzed by one's lack of obedience rather than Jesus' perfect obedience.

In Romans 7, Paul gave himself a very candid "I" exam in his writing. No less than forty times he spoke in the first person, using terms such as *I, me,* and *my* over and again. In every case it had to do with how poorly he had succeeded in keeping the commands of the Law. This was manifested in his lack of progress, for he confessed he constantly was doing the very things he did not want to do. Yet, in the beginning of chapter eight, Paul changes gears, and places the attention from off of his self to that of Jesus and the grace of God. He glories in the Justification that comes through Christ and speaks to the work of the Holy Spirit that results. He makes a personal example of himself to us, displaying that the work of God's Spirit comes through taking our eyes off of our "I" and putting them squarely on what Jesus has accomplished on our behalf. For "I" problems come from "I" exams but true maturity comes from beholding the Lamb of God Who takes away our sin.

More than enough. Those three words characterize Canaan, a land that offered this to God's people. He told them they would not just get by, but that there would be an abundance as characterized by the description, "a land flowing with milk and honey." The concept of a land flowing was far different than the land of Egypt, from which they had come out of. In Egypt they had to grind it out and pump water from the ground. The four hundred years spent in Egypt were characterized by mortar and bricks; they were dependent on their own efforts under the taskmasters of Egypt. Unlike Egypt, Canaan offered the freedom of being dependent on the work of another rather than their own. The Lord promised to them a land that was already established for them, with houses they did not build and vineyards they did not plant. It was a land flowing for it had wells that were already primed and ready. In other words, it was finished. Their job was simply to believe the territory was theirs and to live and act like it was theirs. For the Christ, peace, joy, healing, and blessing are ready are waiting, just as ripe as the cluster of grapes that were the vintage of Canaan. All you have to do is get those grapes by believing that you do not take the territory: you believe it is already taken.

Not enough. That is the condition of God's people in Egypt. Initially, the Pharaoh was a blessing, a means of provision for Israel and his twelve sons through the favor of God upon Joseph. But four hundred years later, the position of blessing that Pharaoh had occupied become a burden to God's people. The book of Galatians tells us that Egypt symbolically is a picture of the Law of God. The Law itself is a blessing. It is so beautiful, though, that it becomes a burden simply through our inability to keep the conditions for the blessing. No matter how well one might adhere to the Law, like Pharaoh and his taskmasters, the Law will always demand more. It accepts nothing short of perfection in order to attain the righteousness required for blessing. The fact is, "all have sinned and fallen short of God's glory."

Standing on the Oregon Coast, we might have a contest in which whoever is able to leap from Oregon to Japan, traversing the Pacific Ocean in a single bound, is the winner. In our attempts to do so, you may have jumped an entire foot further than I. But that distance is negligible due to the sheer distance that still remains. No matter how many good works one does or commands one keeps in order to justify themselves, it is all irrelevant because of the enormity of the chasm between each of us and the standard that perfection demands. As Israel built pyramids and cities for Pharaoh, they never received a single day of rest because the work was never complete. They may as well never even commenced building projects as far as ever receiving reward for their labor. Often Christians just give up and walk away from the faith because they are striving to be righteous through the taskmaster of the Law. Jesus likened this kind of Christian to the seed that was planted in shallow soil yet had no root so that when the heat of the day set in, the plant withered. This is the Christian that makes the fatal mistake of thinking that grace alone got them in the door of the Kingdom but the Law pushes them ahead. They wither under the blistering demands that are self imposed through misappropriating something that never was supposed to rule over them; this is, the Law of God. There is only one means to staying rooted in the Faith, able to withstand the ups and downs that are par for the course in any Christian journey, the Finished work of the Cross. Anything else is not enough.

Just enough. This is what Israel had in the time they spent wandering in the desert between Egypt and Canaan. For forty years, they just got by, or, in other words, had just enough. God faithfully provided bread from heaven that was temporary, dissolving if not immediately picked up and consumed. While the manna speaks of many things, this the context of this analogy it speaks of the stage in our Christian journey where we are out of the Land of Not Enough, which is the Law, and have yet to enter the Land of More than Enough, which is Grace. It's the state of Graw, which is the mixture of Law and Grace. Sadly, it is here that entire church congregations spend forty years at a time. The wilderness, or Graw, is the mindset that one is saved by grace but blessed by performance. Too often, the common error in preaching and in believing is that we are justified by faith yet sanctified by effort. I believe that is where most Christians are today. I do not say that condescendingly because I also believe that we all spend part of lives there, and in fact, even part of each day. Without exception, due to the tendency of human nature to want to take matters into our own hands, we must all labor to enter the rest that comes from the Finished work of the Cross.

In the wilderness of being between Law and Grace, a Christian has just enough. Sadly, that is not what God intends for His children when it comes to the abundant, overflowing life that Jesus speaks about. Case in point is the manna. It met the hunger of every person in proportion to their hunger, no more and no less. Yet in Galilee, Jesus miraculously fed the people with bread to the point they were filled and had twelve baskets of bread left over. This shows how Jesus, our Bread of Life, came not to bring mere existence but a quality of life that is overflowing in blessing. His offering one the Cross was not just enough but so perfect that it not only canceled your debt but purchased every spiritual blessing in heavenly places. The Finished work of the Cross was more than enough when it came to the Law and its demands for your righteousness. Now there lies before us a land flowing with blessing and abundance, more than we could possibly contain in ourselves. All we need to do is rest and believe.

One of my favorite scenes in a Peter Pan flick is in the movie *Hook*, starring Robin Williams as Peter Pan. In this rendition of Neverland, Williams' Peter Pan comes back as an older man, having left many years before. Now cynical and jaded, he has none of the former playfulness nor the power to fly as the young Peter Pan had possessed. While he was sits at the massive dining table with the Lost Boys, the kids who never had left and therefore remained the same age, he was perplexed by the lack of food on the table. All the wares for eating were set before him and the boys were evidently eating heartily from the plates and drinking from the cups. Yet it was as though they were eating literally nothing at all. The moment he believes, though, he is able to see the incredible feast that is actually present and has been there all along. It is his cynicism that kept him from enjoying what was on the table. He couldn't partake in what he did not believe. (Here I have to get ahead of myself and speak to Heaven, which is the last "Rest Stop" of this book. For Heaven is something that one can only partake in if one believes. Heaven on Earth is the same). The blessing and abundance of God's promises in this life are there and have been all along. Like Canaan, it's just a matter of believing it to be in order to be enjoyed.

One reason Canaan was the land of More than Enough was precisely because of the rest it offered. For the first time in four hundred years, the people of God would have a Sabbath. The Sabbath Day was a declaration of independence for Israel. One day a week, by taking a day to do nothing, the people were effectively telling the world they were no longer slaves. In every area of their lives, they were able to do as God had on His day of rest and speak to what they had been working in that, "It is good." When God rested, he was making a statement to His creation. He was telling it that it was good and not needing it to declare that over Him. In other words, God was showing the creation Who was Boss. He made creation and it was not creation that made Him. A Sabbath is afforded to us all when we rest in the fact that we are not made by what we do. We may define it but it does not define us is the statement we are making when we take a day and rest. Even more than a day, the Sabbath is a condition of the soul that breaks us free from the slavery of laboring to make our case for righteousness.

Contentment is a major factor in the land of More than Enough. When Israel was able to rest, they were not only reminding themselves that they were free from the slavery of doing more but also from the slavery of having more. The ability to rest in something and say it is enough actually creates the mindset and atmosphere of more than enough. Jesus taking a few loaves of bread and blessing them was the catalyst for the more than enough in the miracle that followed. The truly wealthy person does not gain everything they desire so much as has less desires. The Finished work of the Cross is able to say over us that we can not only rest from having to do more but from simply having more. This is because we are already complete in the Sabbath of the soul that states, "It is good." John Newton rightly said that the Gospel makes "the worst things in life live-able and the best things in life leave-able." This is because my righteousness is not based on what I have as well as not achieved by what I do. My net worth does not determine my self-worth nor my riches constitute my righteousness under the Finished work of the Cross. My righteousness is found outside of those things. Money is just money and is not my identity. Titles and positions do not make me who I am when I am resting in the Sabbath that Jesus invites me to. In that regard, not only is the Finished work of the Cross more than enough through what is supplied, but also I that I rest in what I already have.

The same way one leaves behind the land of "Not Enough" is the way by which a person enters the land of "More than Enough". Just as the people of Israel exited Egypt through the miraculous parting of the waters, they also entered Canaan by the same. Forty years after passing through the Red Sea, Joshua led the people through the parted waters of the Jordan River and into the Land of Promise. The same way we were first born again is also the way that we mature and grow in our Christian journey. It is all, simply and completely, by rest. Trusting in the Finished work of the Cross. One never "moves on" from it. It is not the starting point, it is the only point. The way out of the desert of just enough is to move beyond Graw and into the territory of God's blessing through the believing that it is not territory that you must take. It is territory that has already been taken in the Finished work of the Cross.

Rest Stop 6: The City of Jerusalem

Jerusalem Above, is it is called by the Apostle Paul, is a city that comes down from heaven as a "bride prepared for her husband", according to the book of Revelation. Jerusalem on Earth is a city that has no recorded beginning but is introduced into the storyline of Scripture as having already been built and established. The Bible is a tale of two cities. While the city of Jerusalem is one having already been built and established, the city of Babylon is given great attention to its initial building and is a city that is never completed. The reason one city is forever finished and the other is perpetually incomplete is because of what lies at the center of each city.

In Genesis, the cities of Jerusalem and Babylon make their initial appearance at roughly the same time. Babylon begins as a tower and the purpose of the building of that tower is explicitly stated by those who built it. "Let us make a name for ourselves" was the mantra of the builders of the Tower of Babel. God came down to the tower, stifled the tower's construction, and scattered the people by confusing their dialect. At the center of Babylon is a monument to man's achievement, a tower that stands forever incomplete. At the center of Jerusalem is a Temple that stood on a hill called Zion. It is Zion where God has declared His Name to be established forever. Zion is also known as Moriah and was the place that Abraham offered his son to God and where the Son of God offered His life. It was on Zion that the Spirit of God came down on the Day of Pentecost and gave the Apostles languages that all people could understand, thereby uniting a people called the Church. Both the Tower of Babel and the Temple on the Mountain are more than physical structures, even as both Jerusalem and Babylon are more than physical cities. Babylon pertains to a system based on making a name while Zion, i.e. Jerusalem, is a kingdom based on the Finished work of the Cross.

The Bible uses both Egypt and Babylon as metaphors for slavery. Paul states Egypt is a picture of our bondage to the Law in terms that no matter how much we labor, if we base our righteousness on our adhering to the Law it will be such a demanding taskmaster we will never find rest. If Egypt speaks of slavery to the Law, Babylon speaks of slavery to the world. Its existence is based on one attempting to establish their own identity through building one's own name. Babylon is about image, brand, and self righteousness through success in the system. Like Egypt, we will never find freedom through using Babylon as a means for righteousness. It is likened to a beast; one that is always consuming until it consumes the very one that is riding it. The number that identifies Babylon is 666. Six being the number of human endeavors based on the day of Creation that man was made and placed in the Garden. The repetition of six is because it is an endless cycle of motion, there is no rest. On the other hand, the number of Heavenly Jerusalem is seven. It stands alone for it speaks of completion, perfection, and to the Finished work of the Cross. It was the Seventh Day of Creation that God brought forth a perpetual Sabbath and stands in stark contrast to the restlessness of Babylon.

For the people of God, the way out of Babylon is the same as it is for Egypt, which is rest. And by rest, it is the resting in the Finished work of the Cross. To put it in the terms of the Old Testament, it is a Sabbath. We already considered that the Sabbath was a declaration of independence for God's people upon their freedom from Egypt. The same is true for Babylon.

By resting on the Sabbath, we are declaring that Babylon does not define us. Babylon does not make us nor give us our name. By resting on the Sabbath Day, we are refusing to buy into a system that demands we make our case for righteousness through how we do in it. As wonderful as that Sabbath rest is, it is more than a day but it is an entire way of life that Jesus bought when He completed the work of the Cross.

In 605 BC, the people of Jerusalem were carried off into exile by the Babylonians. For the next seventy years they lived within the borders of Babylon, the Belly of the Beast. God gave the specific reason as to why He allowed this to happen in the book of 2 Chronicles. He stated that the reason Jerusalem was swallowed up and taken captive by Babylon was because the people of Jerusalem had failed to keep the Sabbath and had not given the land the rest that it needed. The hearts of God's people were captured by Babylon long before Jerusalem was.

The people refused the land its rest and so God "made the land rest" according to the Scripture. Sometimes when we wander away from resting in the Finished work of the Cross, God will allow Babylon to force us to rest. By that I mean that circumstances are no longer in our control and we are unable to make things happen. It might be financially or in a relationship. It could be health or a career. But if we are not resting in the Finished work of the Cross, God is a Shepherd that loves us so much and in His wisdom sees such futility in Babylon, that He will "make" us lie down in green pastures.

Centering our lives around the Sabbath is the way we keep from being sucked into the system. The Finished work of the Cross gets us off the treadmill of trying to make our own name and forge our own identity. Interestingly, the first king of Babylon was a hunter, in the book of Genesis. This pictures the very fabric of the culture of Babylon, one that is preying on the weak and seeking to always attain more. On the other hand, the first king of Jerusalem was a priest. He is seen with bread and wine in his hands instead of a bow and arrow, as was in the hands of Babylon's king. The first king of Jerusalem shows us that the Kingdom of God is based on what is accomplished and not what we need to do. It is not the mindset of a hunter but that of a sacrifice, laying down one's life for the sake of another.

The common thread between Babylon and Jerusalem is a man named Abraham. In Genesis, he forever links the two cities by his journey of faith out of Babylon and headed west, not even knowing where he was headed as he set out. God had simply told him, "Go west, old man" and he did. Once in Canaan, God promised Abraham the land to his descendants though Abraham had no son of his own. When Abraham struggled to believe this, God set up the framework for a covenant. Abraham split up the corpses of the livestock creating a blood path, which was critical to the making of a covenant in those times. For each party of the agreement was deadly serious in keeping the terms. And the concept was meeting in the middle.

Rest Stop 7: The House of the Father

From the Garden of Eden, all the way through the journey of Scripture, the destination of all things is found in something that is prepared and complete. Ready for God's people to simply step into. Such is the case with Heaven, something Jesus referred to as the "Father's House." Jesus told us that it was *He* that would go and prepare a place for us in the Father's House, meaning that is according to His work and not ours. Further, as far as Heaven is concerned, it is already finished and ready for us right now. New Jerusalem is as a "bride prepared for her groom", according to Revelation. The reason is has taken two thousand years for Jesus to prepare Heaven for me is that it takes that long to prepare me for Heaven!

I know of a man who bought a new Mercedes Benz. Up to that point, he had driven an older Chevy car and put a bunch of miles on it. When his teenage daughter obtained her driver's license, he offered to let her drive the Chevy because it was a stick shift and he wanted her to learn how to drive it. She obviously had her sights on the Mercedes. The Mercedes was an automatic transmission and he told her that if she finally figured out how to master the manual transmission, he *might* let her drive the Mercedes. Driving the automatic transmission would be easy because she had mastered the manual one and therefore he could trust her with it. These days we spend on this earth, in these bodies, are like that older Chevy. We are learning the gears as we put on the miles but it will all contribute to the "Mercedes" that awaits us in our resurrection. When Jesus stated that in His Father's house are many rooms and he is going to prepare a pace for you and I, I believe the real preparation is in teaching us how to "get it in gear" when it comes to appropriating and trusting in the Finished work of the

Cross. He is preparing us to step into and enjoy that which has been prepared for us.

Of all the descriptions that Jesus might have used to communicate what lies beyond the grave, He chose to use "My Father's House." The Father's House is where, when we arrive, we will finally be able to say, "I am home." It has been said, "Home is the place that when you get there, they have to let you in." Heaven will "have to let us in" is the implication that Jesus is making it by calling it our Father's House. No one has to let you as when you are family. There are places you might go where you are accepted by folks do not genuinely know you. There are places you might go where you are genuinely known and on that basis folks don't accept you. But in the Father's House, you will be both known and accepted on a genuine basis because that basis is on the Finished work of the Cross. And on that basis alone does Heaven "have to let you in".

We may wonder if we will recognize and know one another in heaven as we do here on earth. That answer is only to the extent we recognize and know each other here as we will there. By that I mean; we will see each other forever under the glory of the Finished work of the Cross. Unlike here, we will see only the beauty and what is complete about each other on the other side. In other words, we will see each other like we have never seen each other before. Even when it came to Jesus' own resurrection, His closet friends and followers did not immediately recognize Him when they saw Him for the first time. He even walked seven miles with two of His disciples before they finally recognized it was Jesus they were walking with and talking to.

In Heaven, we will see each other without superficialities or guarded barriers. There will be no need for hypocrisy for we will only see each other in the perfection of the Finished work of the Cross. CS Lewis went so far as to say if you could see the person sitting next to you at church in the glorified state of what they shall one day be, you would be tempted to bow down and worship them right then and there. (I would add that includes your husband and teenager). Here on Earth we see each other as a work-in-progress, at best, and a piece of work, at worst. God sees us now as we will one day be. And one day, we will see each other in that same light. Mature faith allows us to do that with each other right now.

Have you ever attended a memorial service for something that you knew and the things said about that person didn't seem to line up with who you knew that person to be? As though it was the memorial service for the wrong person? The reason is that when a person passes, only that which is good is remembered and brought to light. I have yet to attend or officiate a memorial service that highlighted the worst of a person. The junk seems to fade away and all that is good remains. Just as God sees in us, we will only see in each other what is good and right. This is because the junk gets burned away in the presence of God.

I believe that the only difference between the presence of God being heaven and the presence of God being hell is the Finished work of the Cross. Heaven is not home because it is where the heart is. Heaven is home because it is where Jesus is. For the only thing that makes Heaven what it is, is Jesus.

God's presence is beautiful. So beautiful, in fact, that it will crush is in its absolute beauty and truth. Isaiah saw a vision of the hem of God's robe fill the temple. Just the glimpse of that alone caused Isaiah to cry out, "Woe is me, I am falling apart!" When encountering the presence of God's holiness, Isaiah did not say, "Wow is me, I sure have my act together!" In that moment he was so aware of the chasm between his reality and the Ultimate Reality that is God, he knew it was too much for him and he fell apart. An angel took a burning coal from off the altar and cauterized the lips of Isaiah, as was noted about the coals of Jesus and Peter by Galilee. God's presence apart from the altar is so beautiful that it is hell itself.

God is fire. Fire does not conform, it does the conforming. Unlike other elements such as water that can change states, fire does not change. In our modern vernacular, it is what it is. God is Who God is. His very name is I Am that I Am. He is ultimate reality and as such, does not change but only does the changing. He does not adjust to us but we adjust to Him as Truth if we want to live. To come face to face with truth is a terrible proposition for you and I. With no censor, no edit, simple candid judgment from that which is True is more terrifying than we realize; unless we are covered with the Truth of the Finished work of the Cross. Then the fire that might otherwise consume us now warms and blesses us. The book of Jude states that on That Day when we stand before God, Jesus will present us before the throne with joy and excitement. So that John tells us we have boldness and confidence concerning standing before God on That Day. Note, Jesus will not present us to God with hesitation and trembling, but with pure joy, as a proud dad with his infant child, or a mother introducing her beautiful daughter to a prospective husband, truly proud and with great excitement. It's one thing for me to point to Jesus and say, "I'm with Him". But on That Day, He is going to actually point to me and say, "He's with Me." Hallelujah, for it is then the Presence of God will not be absolute Hell but the basking in the glow of God's fire.

72

In 2 Thessalonians 1, Paul states, "When the Lord Jesus is revealed from heaven with his mighty angels in a flaming fire, inflicting vengeance upon those who do not know God and on those who do not obey the Gospel of our Lord Jesus. They will suffer the punishment of eternal destruction away from the presence of the Lord and from the glory of His might." We read that what makes the fires of Hell is the absence of the presence of the Lord. Note Whom it is in the text when talking about being separated from the Lord and in the fires of vengeance; the "Lord" in the text is Jesus. What makes the fires of Hell what they are, is not the absence of God but the absence of Jesus in the presence of God. The fire of God without Jesus will consume me. The fire of God with Jesus will save and bless me throughout eternity. As Luther once said, "I hide from God in God." God so loved us and wanted us to be in His presence. He knew the only way that would be possible was to send His Son to accomplish the Finished work of the Cross. Such an accomplishment is our shelter and such a Savior is our mediator not just once we arrive at Heaven's gate, but every moment from then on; which makes it the celebration of the Finished work of the Cross that it truly is.

The same principle for Jesus' presence in eternity is true for when we are going through what Peter calls "fiery trials" here on Earth. The difference between a fiery trial being Heaven or Hell on Earth is the consciousness of Jesus being with me as I go through it. The original Three Amigos, Shadrach, Meshach, and Abednego were in the fiery furnace of Babylon but had to be ordered out of it. It was as though they were enjoying their time in the fire to the point of losing awareness they were in it at all. Just as they, we can not only survive but thrive in the fires we walk through as we are aware of presence of Jesus with us.

My teenage daughter recently traveled to Israel with her grandparents. One of her favorite memories was being at the Garden Tomb in Jerusalem. Just outside the city walls, there is a beautiful little park area in which many scholars suggest is the location of the tomb Jesus' body was placed in after He was taken from the Cross. When she was there, she noted that there were people from all around the world worshipping. There were a variety of languages in which the songs were being sung, and because of that she could not understand the words they were singing. But what she did recognize was the tune of each song. They may have sung in a different language, but everyone was singing the same song. Standing near the tomb, she experienced a small preview of what it will be like on the other side of the grave. People from all different languages, cultures, and nations will gather around the throne and, to each one of us there, we will be singing a song of which we know the tune. It is the Song of Redemption, and it is based on the Finished work of the Cross. What will make Heaven what it is will be all our focus placed upon the Lamb.

When a person came to the Temple in the Old Testament, the priest would inspect the quality of the lamb to see whether the lamb was spotless and if the lamb was worthy. It had nothing to do with the sinner making the offering. All that was evaluated was the offering. In Heaven, the song we will sing is "Worthy is the Lamb!" All of us placing our attention on the beauty of the Lamb and the Finished work of the Cross. The Bible strongly exhorts us not to judge and evaluate one another. Yet in Heaven, we will spend all eternity evaluating and judging the Lamb, each time coming to this conclusion, "Holy, Holy, Holy."

The song we'll forever sing is a bit like the song that Orpheus played in Homer's *Odyssey*. In that legendary tale, the mythological sea nymphs known as the Sirens would direct their enchanting songs from the island to each ship sailing by. The song would lure the soldiers toward the rocks near the island and destroy the boats. One after another, captains would steer their vessels into oblivion, contrary to their natural marine instincts, as they could not resist the song of the Sirens. Odysseus sought to overcome the Siren's song using means through which many today use to stave off the Siren Song of Temptation. He had his men bind him to the mast of the ship so it was impossible for him to head toward the Sirens' song even if he wanted to. His men placed wax in their ears and were able to successfully sail by the island without being destroyed. However, Orpheus was able to overcome the song of the Sirens using something more beautiful than even their song. As his ship sailed by the island, instead of being bound to the mast as Odysseus or having wax placed in the ears of his men, Orpheus matched the beauty of their song and surpassed it with music from his fiddle. It was such a beautiful sound that proceeded from the captain, his men were able to sail by the island without being swayed whatsoever by the song of the Sirens.

The Song of Redemption is sweeter than any the world has to offer. Nothing in Babylon can compare. Instead of tying ourselves down, being bound by the Law, we are justified and set free to sail through the Finished work of the Cross. "It is Finished" is the inspiration and basis for the most beautiful song the world has ever known.

At the center of New Jerusalem is Eden. At the center of Eden is God's throne. Around God's throne is a sea that is so calm it is described by John as "glass." When we are aware of the Finished work of the Cross, and find our rest even as Christ has found His seat, there can be no longer stormy conditions and choppy waters. The disciples saw this first hand on the waters of Galilee. "Master, you don't even care that we are going to drown!" They shook Jesus Who was sleeping in the hull of the boat. Jesus stepped up and spoke to the storm, calming it to the point that it had a "mega-calm" in the original language of the text. I like to imagine in my mind the waves stopping so suddenly and completely, they were not even bobbing up against the side of the boat. How I'd love to see the look on the faces of the disciples, as the Gospel tells us they were "astonished." In the center of the storm, what they did not realize was that Jesus wasn't asleep on the job. He was resting in the boat. They mistook Jesus' resting for sleeping.

When we rest in the Finished work of the Cross, we are resting in the very thing that Jesus is resting in. Jesus is not asleep in the midst of your storm. In fact, He is so in control, that the calmness of His demeanor and lack of hyperactivity might just give you the impression He is checked out of the situation. Jesus is not checked out. Jesus is sitting down. If you are resting in your ability to make things happen or to take matters in your own hands, you will not get very much rest. But if you are resting in what Jesus is resting in, the crazy conditions of the storm will give way to the mega-calm in your heart. All Jesus did when calming storm with His word was manifested outwardly what He had within Himself. And when you rest within, the storm outside will surely follow the calm you are experience inside. Knowing that Jesus is so confident that you are going to make it through the Finished work of the Cross that He is seated in a place of rest, gives us rest as well. And having rest in the soul, no matter what fiery trials or stormy situations we are navigating our way through, is having heaven come down into our hearts.

The Final Word

"It is Finished". That was the final word of Jesus when He breathed His very last. It was His final word. And it has the last word over your sin, over your past, and over your life.

Made in the USA
San Bernardino, CA
20 August 2016